Instructor's Manual

to accompany

Goshgarian/Krueger/Minc

DIALOGUES:

An Argument Rhetoric and Reader

Fourth Edition

Kathryn A. Goodfellow

Harvard Medical School

Longman

New York Boston San Francisco
London Toronto Sydney Tokyo Singapore Madrid
Mexico City Munich Paris Cape Town Hong Kong Montreal

NOTE REGARDING WEB SITES AND PASSWORDS:

If you need a password to access instructor supplements on a Longman book-specific Web site, please use the following information:

Username: awlbook
Password: adopt

Instructor's Manual to accompany Goshgarian/Krueger/Minc, *Dialogues: An Argument Rhetoric and Reader, 4th Edition*

Copyright ©2003 Pearson Education, Inc.

ISBN: 0-321-10709-8

2 3 4 5 6 7 8 9 10–DPC–05 04 03 02

CONTENTS

PREFACE

Dialogues: An Argument Rhetoric and Reader, Fourth Edition, encourages students to explore multiple perspectives on a particular issue to enable them to formulate their own opinions and prepare their own arguments. Part One of the text addresses how to evaluate, assess, analyze and build arguments through critical reading and comparing and synthesizing viewpoints. It also examines the different types of arguments and the ways visuals can be used to support a claim and persuade an audience. Part Two of the text addresses topical arguments focusing on specific issues or questions, encouraging students to experience multiple points of view. Many of the questions in Part Two are designed to facilitate a synthesis of perspectives held on a wide variety of valuable social, political, and intellectual topics.

This instructor's manual provides answers to the questions in the book. In addition to providing information and possible responses to the questions, many answers provide suggestions for class discussion and references for more information.

The book's Companion Website, *Dialogues on the Web*, (www.ablongman.com/goshgarian) includes additional class activities and questions, topical resources, links to research and reference pages, online writing labs, and updates to links listed in the book. It also features an extensive "Instructor Resources" section providing teaching, writing, and research links. Please contact your textbook representative for more information about Daedalus Online, or for additional ancillary materials.

In addition to the Companion Website, ask your representative about Course Compass, Pearson Education's course management system, free to adopters of our content. Course Compass provides flexible tools and rich content resources that enable you to easily and efficiently customize Pearson Online Content to best suit your needs.

CHAPTER ONE
UNDERSTANDING PERSUASION: THINKING LIKE A NEGOTIATOR

TAKING A "WAR OF WORDS" TOO LITERALLY

1. Instead of exploring the many facets of an issue, Tannen points out
    that the media prefers to make everything a battle. Controversy sells
    and conflict is interesting. The problem is that by assuming a polar
    position and defending it to the death, we close our ears to other points
    of view. It becomes a situation where everyone is talking and no one is
    listening. Newspapers employ provoking and often adversarial
    headlines designed to stir up reader interest. Reporters endeavor to
    reveal all the hidden dirt on a public figure – rarely highlighting positive
    things the individual may have done. Class discussion may include a
    discussion regarding the political battles currently taking place in
    Congress, or Enron and its possible connections to the White House.

    News media isn't the only culprit here. Most television talk shows
    feature adversarial confrontations like the one featured in Tannen's
    article. Shows like *the Jerry Springer Show* almost skip discussion
    entirely in favor of getting down to the physical blows. It would seem
    there is no room for middle ground as long as there is a market for
    fighting.

2. By taking sides, we may block out any reasonable perspective the
    other side may present. In other words, we prevent consensus. Gun
    control could be one example. One side says ban all handguns (guns
    kill people), and the other says we have the constitutional right to bear
    arms (people kill people). Neither side wants to listen to the other,
    and very little progress has been made on the issue because no one is
    willing to give up any "ground." The essay by Jack Levin in Chapter
    15 addresses this very issue.

3. Student answers will vary.

4. Debate is often encouraged in many classrooms, especially in higher education. While the objective is usually to encourage discussion, argument is often the end result. The problem is that once arguments get really going, it is difficult to return the class to a more objective and thoughtful level. In some cases, students may become so angered at each other that shouting matches result. Tannen points out that this method of inquiry prevents productive discussion and eliminates the possibility for consensus.

The "winner-take-all" approach to arguments may prevent meaningful dialog. The inflexibility of this approach rarely solves the problem. In a situation where somebody "wins" and somebody "loses," there is bound to be resentment. In your effort to get your point across, you may forget the central issues and alternative viewpoints. Moreover, when one side feels that they have lost, they are unlikely to adopt the "winning" point of view anyway.

SAMPLE ARGUMENTS FOR ANALYSIS

THE CASE AGAINST TIPPING

1. Tipping has become an obligatory practice in which patrons are shamed or bullied into rewarding a service, no matter how good or poor that service is. Lewis wants to alert readers to this growing trend in our society, perhaps to motivate a change in behavior.

2. Lewis points out several reasons why tipping is bad. A) It may be abused by employers who will reduce wages in anticipation of the tip augmenting the employee's income. B) Tipping has its roots in "aristocratic conceit" in which the rich bestow money on those who

serve them. C) It becomes so expected that some service people may retaliate when not given a good tip, regardless of the quality of service. D) The more expected a tip becomes, the less likely the server will work harder to earn it.

3. Lewis presents several examples from his own experience to support his claims. He starts his essay with the coffee shop/cup-on-the-counter scenario. He also presents the problems with New York City cab drivers. His examples may be considered a bit slanted because he does not account for situations in which stellar service should be rewarded. All of his examples present scenarios of little or poor service.

4. In his endeavor to present his argument, Lewis leaves little room for an alternative viewpoint. When he does "present" the opposite side, he is very negative. Using the phrase "offensively rich people may delight in peeling off hundred-dollar bills..." may not be fair to those individuals who approve of tipping. It also questions the sincerity of people who are generous with their money. And comparing the taxi cab driver to the counter cup isn't exactly a parallel situation.

5. Peer group work.

THE CONSEQUENCES OF "CARNAGE AS ENTERTAINMENT"

1. Ellis believes that violent television and movies desensitize children to the realities of violence and encourages violent behavior. Ellis hopes to alert readers to this trend in our culture and correct it before it is too late.

2. Ellis provides reasons why we should be concerned about television violence. A) Children learn that extremely violent behavior, such as shooting one's classmates, receives extensive media coverage. They

may get the idea that committing such acts will get them national attention and fame. B) Violent programming now dominates prime time television as well as film. C) Television violence is getting worse. D) Researches claim that there is a direct link between violence in the media and violent behavior in children.

3. Ellis uses the actual reports of school shooting to introduce his essay: five shootings in a seven-month time period. He also presents statistical data regarding violence in television programming in paragraphs 10-12. Ellis may be making unfair comparisons.

In the beginning of the article, Ellis seems to imply that it is the news-coverage of the violent school shootings that encourage youth to commit violent acts operating under the belief that they will be "rewarded" fame and media coverage. He does not consider other reasons why youths may act out violent impulses. For most of the essay, he blames television programming and movies for violent trends. But are news reports of violence in the same category as violent movies?

4. Ellis expresses disbelief and outrage at the opposition's view. Specifically, he attacks Jack Valenti, president of the Motion Picture Association of America. He calls Valenti's opinion "irresponsible" leaving little doubt as to the writer's opinion of his opponents.

5. Peer group work.

QUESTIONS FOR DISCUSSION AND WRITING

THE CASE AGAINST TIPPING

1. Student answers will vary.

2. Student answers will vary.

THE CONSEQUENCES OF "CARNAGE AS ENTERTAINMENT"

1. Student answers will vary.

2. Student answers will vary.

3. Ellis presents an "either - or" argument. He tells us that we must either fix the current problem, or face the end of civilization as we know it. Ellis is guilty of logical fallacy in that he provides little proof that media violence is truly going to cause the destruction of civilization. A better tactic may be to simply highlight the increase in violent behavior in children and suggest a correlation between this behavior and violent programming in the news, television programming, and films. He should also address other reasons for violent behavior in children, such as increased availability of firearms, drug use, peer pressure, and reduced parental guidance at home.

CHAPTER END EXERCISES

1.
a) arguable
b) arguable
c) not arguable
d) not arguable
e) arguable
f) arguable
g) not arguable
h) not arguable
i) arguable
j) not arguable
k) arguable
l) arguable
m) arguable
n) arguable
o) arguable
p) arguable
q) not arguable
r) arguable

2. Student answers will vary.

3. Student answers will vary.

4. Student answers will vary.

*Please reference the book's Companion Website, **Dialogues on the Web**, at (www.ablongman.com/goshgarian) for additional class activities and questions, topical resources, links to research and reference pages, online writing labs, and updates to links listed in the book. Also see its "Instructor Resources" section providing teaching, writing, and research links.*

CHAPTER TWO
READING ARGUMENTS: THINKING LIKE A CRITIC

1.
   a. *ad hominem*
   b. *non sequitur*, begging the question
   c. slippery slope, *ad populum*
   d. non sequitur
   e. red herring and *ad homineum*
   f. false analogy
   g. *non sequitur*
   h. circular reasoning
   i. hasty generalization, and *post hoc, ergo propter hoc*
   j. false analogy
   k. stacking the deck
   l. *ad populum*

*Please reference the book's Companion Website, **Dialogues on the Web**, at (www.ablongman.com/goshgarian) for additional class activities and questions, topical resources, links to research and reference pages, online writing labs, and updates to links listed in the book. Also see its "Instructor Resources" section providing teaching, writing, and research links.*

CHAPTER THREE
FINDING ARGUMENTS: THINKING LIKE A WRITER

There are no questions that need to be answered in this chapter for the Instructor's Manual.

CHAPTER FOUR
ADDRESSING ARGUMENTS: THINKING LIKE A READER

SAMPLE ARGUMENTS FOR ANALYSIS

DON'T FORGET THE SMOKERS

1. Author's Claims/Points: In our effort to prevent teenagers from smoking, we must not forget older smokers who still need our attention and assistance. Cigarettes are addictive. Tobacco companies know and count on this. Tobacco companies are trying to fight the FDA's regulation of cigarette marketing. The FDA's authority over tobacco must not be undermined.

2. Koop assumes the audience will understand the urgency of his message, and agree that cigarettes are bad for personal and public health. He also presumes that his audience understands some medical terminology, is fairly literate, and is informed of current political lobbying activities by the big tobacco companies.

3. Koop uses words like "Big Tobacco" and implies that tobacco companies are conspiring against the public health. He also accuses them of employing reverse psychology in their last campaign "against" teen smoking. He presents a very negative picture of his opponents, but does so in a very methodical and well-supported way. He tries to back up his claims with evidence the audience can relate to.

4. Koop is very respectful of his audience. He repeatedly employs inclusive words such as "we" and treats them like equals in his argument against big tobacco companies.

5. This argument is fairly balanced, although it does assume that the audience is of a like mind.

6. Koop establishes common ground quite effectively. He appeals to his audience's desire to protect teens from the clutches of cigarettes and he comments that we should not abandon or forget smokers who want to quit. Both smokers and non-smokers are addressed without accusation or ill will.

7. Koop hopes to enlighten his audience to the lobbying activities of "Big Tobacco."

WHAT THE ANTISMOKING ZEALOTS REALLY CRAVE

1. Author's Claims/Points: Antismoking advocates are infringing on the rights of smokers. Antismoking rhetoric should be more consistent and honest in admitting its objectives.

2. Jacoby is writing *at* an audience of anti-tobacco supporters. At the same time, audience members who are smokers may feel included by knowing that he is defending their rights.

3. Jacoby's argument is not very balanced. It is written from an angry viewpoint, and uses charged language. This is a "me against you" argument.

4. Jacoby's attitude is belligerent and accusing. He is angry and not afraid to let his readers know it.

5. This essay has many logical fallacies, including *ad hominem*, stacking the deck, red herrings and false analogies. Jacoby would have to alter the tone, style and structure of his argument to correct the problems with his editorial.

6. Jacoby's intent is not to establish common ground, but perhaps to highlight some injustice's surrounding the issue.

7. The purpose of this essay is to address the inconsistencies in the anti-tobacco campaign, and highlight its unfair policies and prejudices.

MEDIA HAVE FALLEN FOR THE MISGUIDED ANTISMOKING CAMPAIGN

1. Author's Claims/Points: The media has succumbed to the view promoted by the popular antismoking campaign that smokers are victims lacking free will. Taxing smokers penalizes the poor. Teens are not smoking as much as we think, and hazards of second-hand smoke are questionable. Government, society and even the tobacco industry have abandoned the rights of smokers.

2. Samuelson is addressing a largely neutral audience and assumes that he will be able to appeal to their sense of fairness. He perhaps, however, assumes that they will not carefully examine his presentation of the "facts." This may assume a bit of naïveté on the part of his audience. His comment about cigarette taxation affecting the poor also assumes that they will be sympathetic to this issue.

3. Samuelson tries to appear as if he is presenting a balanced view, but his interpretation and presentation of the data is skewed.

4. Overall, Samuelson's tone is respectful of his audience.

5. Samuelson is guilty of several logical fallacies including red herrings, stacking the deck, and non sequitur. For example, in his attempt to prove that studies give conflicting information, he mentions that in 1996, *only* 18.3 percent of teenagers smoked in the last month, a

13

decrease since 1985. He ignores the fact that still almost 20% of teens smoked at all! He words this as if teen smoking is not a real problem. Another example is his observation that teens do a lot of bad things, so why are we singling out smoking? He is trying to direct the audience from the real issue that teens do smoke. He also withholds statistical data when it doesn't support his argument's goals.

6. Common ground is established in Samuelson's appeal to the smoking poor, and his audience's sense of fairness.

7. To redirect the media's coverage of smoking and to decrease bias in their reporting.

CHAPTER END EXERCISES

1. Student answers will vary.

2. Reasons in favor of claim:
   a. * Snowboarders tend to be young, reckless males who take risks.
       * Snowboarders jeopardize the slopes of family skiers.
       * Snowboarders tend to ski at extreme speeds, with little ability to slow themselves down.
   b. * A 55-mile speed limit will reduce the number of fatal accidents.
       * A 55-mile speed limit allows for more reaction time.
       * A 55-mile speed limit nationwide takes the guesswork out of traveling on highways.
   c. * Advertising condoms on television would help remove embarrassment associated with talking about them.
       * Advertising condoms on television would publicize their benefits.
       * Advertising condoms on television could help reduce STDs.
   d. * Denying federal aid to students with drug convictions sends a clear message to young people of the ramifications of drug use.
       * The government shouldn't have to assist students who break the law.

14

* Students will have a response to peer pressure "I can't, I could lose my loan."

Reasons to oppose claim:
a. * Snowboarding provides a good, athletic outlet for teens.
   * Snowboarders often stay on slopes specifically designated for that purpose.
   * Snowboarders exercise more caution because they know they are monitored closely by the ski patrol.
b. * A 55-mile speed limit is unrealistic, few people drive that slowly.
   * A 55-mile speed limit will increase commuting time.
   * A 55-mile speed limit may increase the number of traffic jams on highways.
c. *Advertising condoms on television may send the message that sexual promiscuity is permissible.
   * Advertising condoms on television may offend some people.
   * Advertising condoms on television could encourage teen experimentation.
d. * Students with a drug conviction shouldn't be penalized for what could be only one mistake.
   * Refusing federal aid could make students drop out of school; less educated people may be more likely to break the law again.
   * Refusing federal aid to students in this category is too vague, isn't there a difference between a drug dealer and a teen who tries pot?

3. Student answers will vary.

4. Student answers will vary.

5. Connotations of words:
a. *Weird*: implies that something is odd or wrong with her choice.
   Exotic: of an intriguing nature and foreign in a positive way.

Unusual: different from the expected, may be good or bad.

b. *Polluting*: gives an impression of chemical and environmental dangers.

Stinking up: a less formal, slang expression implying distaste.

Fouling: a sense of toxicity, dangerous to health.

c. *Unaware*: simply uninformed, doesn't know the facts.

Ignorant: implies stupidity or lack of education.

Unconscious: gives impression of obliviousness to one's surroundings.

d. *Popular*: part of a movement approved by large group and in vogue.

Trendy: a passing fad, not likely to last or without permanence.

Common: part of an established way of thinking.

e. *Stomped*: implies anger, hostility and some level of immaturity.

Marched: seems purposeful, with determination.

Stepped: she simply left.

6.

a. The expression "the Old Country," meaning the country of origin of an immigrant, is a cliché that is also a personification; the country is old. "Slam the door" is another figure of speech, American's cannot literally slam the door on their place of origin, but this sentence has them figuratively doing so.

b. "Racial profiling" is compared to a "tool" – an example of metaphor.

c. The conversation will be *like* a phone conversation with a bad connection, an example of simile.

d. The "beasts" in the sentence are personified by "slouching." And the expression "strange beasts" is a metaphor for materialism.

16

e. These two sentences are full of metaphors and similes—light wanes, trees merge, blackness is velvety, waves rise, and shapes dissolve (all metaphors). The creek froth shines *like* the Milky Way (a simile). All these metaphors are used as an overarching simile for the author himself—"*like* my own body, *like* the mountains, *like* the earth and stars."

f. The hand is personified—scuttles and finds—the author's glasses.

g. The fire is personified (belch). "...as if the ruin" is a simile, compared to a volcano, which is further personified by "spreading" stench.

h. Realism is personified by giving "counsel." "Scot-free" is a cliché.

7. It is not that we are unconcerned with space exploration; it is that many Americans do not understand what these untold billions of dollars can accomplish. While significant advances have been made in space research, we ask ourselves: Is life any safer? Are material goods more abundant? Has the expense extended our life expectancy or improved our overall health? The answer is no. Congressional leaders must realize that the nation's urgent problems of crime, homelessness, and unemployment are here on earth. No government budget should be spared including NASA's. While some people may object to cutbacks, they must remember that our tax dollars are limited. Overall, spending money on space exploration is wasteful.

*Please reference the book's Companion Website, **Dialogues on the Web**, at (www.ablongman.com/goshgarian) for additional class activities and questions, topical resources, links to research and reference pages, online writing labs, and updates to links listed in the book. Also see its "Instructor Resources" section providing teaching, writing, and research links.*

CHAPTER FIVE
SHAPING ARGUMENTS: THINKING LIKE AN
ARCHITECT

QUESTIONS FOR DISCUSSION AND ANALYSIS

SCHOOLS CAN HELP TO PREVENT TEEN PREGNANCY

1. Martha identifies the problem after providing two paragraphs of statistical data and facts to support her claim. She begins by presenting the number of pregnancies in the US and the strain it puts on families, children, and taxpayers. She then states the problem outright in her third paragraph.

2. Martha proposes to solve the problem by implementing an interactive sex education program that encourages parents, teachers, and students to openly communicate. She begins to explain her plan in paragraph 4.

3. Martha touches on the different ways her idea will solve the problem in paragraphs 4 and 5, although she revisits her solution throughout the essay, effectively reminding her audience of her point.

4. In paragraph 7, Martha explains how she hopes her program will work by attacking the problem on two fronts rather than on only one.

5. While Martha admits that some people would object to her solution, she quickly explains that it is not an ideal world where all parents work together with their children. Until it is, we need sex education in the schools. The focus of her essay is not addressing the objections to her plan, but in proposing it.

6. Martha cites how other programs like hers were successful in California where teen pregnancies have dropped. She elaborates and provides statistics on their success in paragraph 7.
7. Martha conveys the mature attitude of a concerned parent. She accounts for alternative points of view, does not accuse any one party of negligence and focuses on problem solving.

CHAPTER END EXERCISES

Questions 1-8
Student answers will vary for this section.

*Please reference the book's Companion Website, **Dialogues on the Web**, at (www.ablongman.com/goshgarian) for additional class activities and questions, topical resources, links to research and reference pages, online writing labs, and updates to links listed in the book. Also see its "Instructor Resources" section providing teaching, writing, and research links.*

CHAPTER SIX
USING EVIDENCE: THINKING LIKE AN ADVOCATE

QUESTIONS FOR DISCUSSION AND ANALYSIS

VIOLENT CULTURE: THE MEDIA, THE INTERNET, AND PLACING THE BLAME

1. Beals argues, or rather, explores the argument, that the Internet played a significant role in creating, reinforcing, and facilitating Kip Kinkel's acts of violence in 1998. Beals wonders if the television media's persistent reporting of a connection between Kinkel's actions and his use of the Internet—a primary competitor of television—is biased, so he decides to personally investigate this assertion.

2. Because this essay was prepared for an expository writing class, Beals' primary audience is presumably his teacher and classmates. It is probable that Beals considered his own peer group when framing his argument. He assumes that his audience is familiar with the nuances of the Internet and is aware of the current trend of blaming the media for teen violence. It is possible that this audience, raised in the same culture as Kinkel (the median age of the class is probably only 3-5 years older than Kinkel) may resist the idea that the media is to blame for violence in teens.

3. Beals uses many different types of supporting evidence. He cites reports in newspapers and programs on television. He refers to his own observations and experience. He provides statistical information from reliable sources, such as the Justice Department. Finally, his own research makes him somewhat of an authority—he refers to what he saw and found during his exploration of the Internet. To support the type of argument he makes in this essay, Beals relies a great deal on personal experience, but backs up this experience whenever possible with outside sources.

21

5. Much of Beals' evidence provides solid support for his essay's claims and observations. While he refers to reports coming from the *Associated Press*, he also cites news-programs of varied authority such as *Face the Nation* and *Dateline* (respected news sources) to *Inside Edition* and *Extra* (tabloid programs). This shows a cross-section of reporting, but may not be equally respected by the reader. His use of evidence gathered from the online *Dateline* quiz is particularly compelling, as well as his acknowledging different opinions—such as the paragraph citing the NRA's comments. To describe Kinkel as compared to other teens, Beals refers to observations made by neighbors, reports made in the media, and his own experience. However, because Beals is not a 15-year-old boy, he may not be truly able to "imagine" what it is like to be Kinkel—a concept on which his argument heavily relies.

Beals does an excellent job in describing his research on the Internet as it relates to his argument and what he is trying to prove. He details the steps he took to uncover information—steps that can be easily repeated by his audience. His conclusions, however, may be questioned and are possibly contradictory in logic. He says that he does not believe that television OR the Internet was to blame for Kinkel's violence, but rather "our national culture of violence" is responsible. Critics could argue that television and the Internet comprise an integral component of American culture, and cannot be separated from overall ideology. To make his argument stronger, Beals should have explained why he feels that television violence is not connected to "national culture."

*Please reference the book's Companion Website, **Dialogues on the Web**, at (www.ablongman.com/goshgarian) for additional class activities and questions, topical resources, links to research and reference pages, online writing labs, and updates to links listed in the book. Also see its "Instructor Resources" section providing teaching, writing, and research links.*

CHAPTER SEVEN
ESTABLISHING CLAIMS: THINKING LIKE A SKEPTIC

FOR ANALYSIS AND DISCUSSION

ARGUING FOR INFANTICIDE

1. Kelley claims that despite his prior belief that abortion would not cause an overall devaluation of human life, Pinker's article, printed in an intellectual media resource (the New York Times) indicates that it indeed has. He then proceeds to explain what was wrong with Pinker's claims and support.

2. Pinker claims that infanticide, in cases such as those recently publicized by the media, are not as morally horrible as we think. Many cultures accept infanticide. Furthermore, mothers instinctually weigh the overall "survival" prospects of the infant when deciding whether to let it live or die. Kelley objects to Pinker's references from "moral philosophers" regarding what makes one human, his hypothesis on how the mind works, and his argument's support by Michael Tooley. Kelley attacks Tooley's reasoning and thus, that of Pinker as well.

3. Kelley largely disregards Pinker's comments on the actions of a few "depressed new mothers" to compare their actions to that of "millions of mothers." This allows Kelley to focus on the "monstrosity" of Pinker's claim. However, Kelley's omission may actually skip a point he should have addressed – that the action of depressed new mothers is one of the mother's perception of her own survival, not that of the infant's.

4. Kelley implies that the legalization of abortion has caused an intellectual and moral shift in American culture typified by the

opinions of people such as Pinker. If Pinker, a respected scientist, believes this, and the New York Times, a respected newspaper, prints it, then it must represent the opinions of a larger population.

5. Kelley's use of words here indicates that he may believe that Pinker is leaving himself an out. By rewording Pinker's warrant this way, he implies to the audience that this is *exactly* what Pinker was advocating.

6. Euphemizing something means you make it sound less harsh, such as saying "she passed away" instead of "she died." Kelley proposes that Pinker took the basic ideas from Tooley's article and made them sound less harsh. This means that Pinker embraces the same ideas as Tooley, he just prettified the language. Kelley reinforces the connection between Pinker and the more radical Tooley by pointing out that Pinker does indeed quote Tooley in his article. Pinker may not actually endorse Tooley's theories, but Kelley makes it sound like he does.

7. Student answers will vary.

8. Student answers will vary.

DID I MISS SOMETHING?

1. Putnam's claim is that divorce hasn't hurt him or affected his well-being, despite the cultural attitude "experts" imply. Student's may agree or disagree with his perspective, depending on their own experience with divorce. How people speak of divorce often depends on their generation—older generations may indeed still discuss it in "lowered tones" while other groups, for whom divorce is perhaps more common, speak of it unabashedly. The topic is even the focus of a television program—"Divorce Court."

2. Putnam bases his claim on personal experience, perhaps the most convincing evidence he could provide. He describes how he has—or hasn't—been emotionally affected by his parents' separation. His description, however, does not acknowledge the opinion of "experts" in the field, who may disagree with his first hand experience, or question his assertions.

3. Student responses will vary, but Putnam does make good use of cultural assumptions here. Most people would agree that love is the fundamental base of good parenting, at least on the surface. Child psychologists may argue, however, that many other factors are equally important—such as discipline, structure, and creating a healthy environment.

4. Again—Putnam's statement taps into a widely-held belief that love is the most important component to a successful parent/child relationship. But are all loving parents successful ones? One could argue that a great many children who abuse drugs, drop out of school, or commit crimes had loving parents. And what about loving parents who cannot even afford to furnish children with basic necessities, let alone "sophisticated gourmet delicacies"? Are they guaranteed success simply because they love their children? Class discussion could cover the elements of what makes a successful parent, and how this success is assessed.

5. Putnam makes many convincing warrants in this essay. A few include 1) love makes a family, 2) a loving parent is a good parent, 3) happy, separated parents are better than married miserable ones, 4) because 60% of marriages end in divorce, a large group of children of divorce make up the "norm," 5) society has "evolved" to better accept and accommodate divorce, 6) benefits of divorce include no parental "double-teaming" and greater appreciation for the time one has with one's parents.

6. This statement, rather than weakening Putnam's essay, serves to make it stronger. He is anticipating some reader rebuttal, and acknowledges that he may seem too "cheerful." He then admits to some difficulties, but frames them in such a way as to explain why these difficulties are not that bad. It is interesting, for example, that when describing how during holidays he is not with one parent, he says that his *parent* is forced to explain, "Lowell is with his father/mother." In other words, he is sensitive to how the situation is difficult for his parents, rather than difficult on him.

7. Throughout his essay, Putnam anticipates rebuttal. For example, he comments that "many people have had lives torn apart" by divorce, and when he admits that divorce means he is always away from one parent half the time. However, he does not seem to anticipate the arguments made by some psychologists who make claims very different from Putnam's. Class research into statistics may provide a forum for rebuttal. For example, are children of divorce more likely to drop out of school? Are they less likely to pursue higher education? Are they more likely to live in poverty? Because Putnam's narrative is based primarily on personal experience, he leaves a great deal of room for statistical and intellectual rebuttal.

8. Student responses will vary.

9. Student responses will vary.

*Please reference the book's Companion Website, **Dialogues on the Web**, at (www.ablongman.com/goshgarian) for additional class activities and questions, topical resources, links to research and reference pages, online writing labs, and updates to links listed in the book. Also see its "Instructor Resources" section providing teaching, writing, and research links.*

CHAPTER EIGHT
VISUAL ARGUMENTS

FOR ANALYSIS AND DISCUSSION

PABLO PICASSO'S "GUERNICA"

1. Student responses will vary.

2. This mural features many "central" figures: the figure with outstretched arms at the right of the painting; the wailing mother at the left; the head emerging from the window at the top; the twisted horse in the center; the arm with the broken sword at the bottom. Because Picasso is presenting many different images that "happen" over a period of time, each image is considered as separate parts of a whole event.

3. The title orients viewers to what is happening in the mural. Without this title, viewers could have inferred the painting's overall meaning, but may have not understood its direct inspiration. Because Picasso wanted his audience to understand what he was depicting, he named the painting after the town that had suffered this horrible event.

4. Almost all the images in the painting are exaggerated, which is in keeping with the style of the work. However, some images stand out more than others. Students may discuss which ones seem to be more prominent and exaggerated, and why.

5. As a black and white mural, Picasso presents war in "frank" terms. The images are stark, color is absent. Students could discuss what this color choice may symbolize, and if the painting would have been different if presented in color.

6. Student responses will vary.

7. We know from Picasso's sketches that he carefully considered each figure in his painting, so we may presume that almost every figure symbolizes something. For example, we know that the bull is a symbol for Spain. At the bottom of the picture, an arm clutches a broken sword. Spanish swords were world renown, as well as Spain's traditions of heroism and honor. But the sword is broken, useless against the destructive force of bombs. The people of Guernica did not have a chance to fight an enemy or defend themselves. The innocent subjects of the painting also relay the idea that cowards—who attacked sleeping people, and killed women and children, perpetrated the attack. Students should discuss what other symbols they see in the painting—such as the meaning of the light bulb at the top of the mural.

NORMAN ROCKWELL'S "SAVE FREEDOM OF SPEECH" POSTER

1. In addition to the standing man, two other faces assume prominence: the two men beside and in front of the standing figure, who look up at him with respect and interest.

2. The central image, as discussed in the text, is the standing man. Students should further discuss Rockwell's reasons for choosing to depict this particular figure in his poster.

3. The poster features a title in capital letters, that tell you what action is taking place in the picture. Ask students how their impression of the painting changes when the poster's title is taken away. Without the title, would the writing at the bottom of the poster make any sense?

4. Facial expressions are emphasized, for emotional impact. The man's face resembles Abraham Lincoln, an idealized president. Even the people themselves represent an idealized image of small town America.

5. The figure stands before a black background, which serves to highlight him. And the use of shadow on his face focuses the viewer's eye on him.

6. Student responses will vary.

7. Symbolism may be implied in the resemblance between the man and Abraham Lincoln. His humble clothing, and the papers in his pocket.

ADVERTISEMENT: TIMBERLAND

1. Because the photograph features two men ice fishing, color is not essential to the success of the ad. Snow and sky make up most of the photo. While it might be nice to have blue sky in the photo, the effect of color would be lost on the snow component of the picture.

2. The ad copy featured at the top of the picture, in the area of the sky, explains what the view is looking at: a father and son are ice fishing and enjoying quality time together. Without the text, the viewer is unable to make the emotional connection.

3. The ad emphasizes connectivity between father and son. It juxtaposes the masculine—the men are dressed ruggedly, braving the elements, fishing—and the sensitive—the father has just shared his dreams with his son. The son has just learned something about his father that he did not know, and his father feels close enough to open up and share his inner hopes with his son.

4. One would presume that the viewer would check "yes" although this is not done in the ad. Would the effect be different if the box was already checked off? The statement "Learned dad had pretty weird dreams" adds humor and lightens the mood.

5. Timberland is known for rugged gear—boots and jackets. It makes sense that the company chose this environment to show off their products.

6. Without the name of the product, you would not know what was being sold in this ad. Moreover, the ad presumes that the viewer will know what Timberland makes. The claims are that Timberland's gear will

keep its wearers warm and dry enough to enjoy the sport of ice fishing, so that they can focus on things like father-son talks.

7. The appeals to people who enjoy the outdoors, of many ages. While women are not included in the ad, the emotional component of a father and son sharing dreams may appeal to a female audience—to both buy the products for the men in their lives and even buy for themselves.

8. While the coats and boots are not given prominence in comparison to the other objects in the picture, the positioning of the two men on the backdrop of white snow and ice emphasizes the product—cold weather gear.

ADVERTISEMENT: CUREL

1. The ad employs the unexpected—a woman who appears to be half human and half tree. Because viewers see something they don't anticipate, they are more likely to look at the ad longer.

2. The target audience is most likely women, over the age of thirty, who the model most likely represents. The economic level and lifestyle is more ambiguous, and this may be on purpose—to appeal to a wide range of consumers. The woman's short haircut, however, has a definite "mom" look about it—no nonsense and practical—and perhaps represents the membership of the primary target audience.

3. The part human/tree image, as mentioned in question 1, surprises the viewer. While not exactly comical, it is likely to strike a chord with women who have dry skin, which can seem to be like dry bark. The ad's use of texture, the juxtaposition of the woman's smooth skin with the dry bark, also ads to the image's central message that Curel will prevent this "condition."

4. Student responses will vary.

5. The central claim is the Curel will cure very dry skin, or at the very least, "fix" it. The text reinforces this idea.

6. Student responses will vary, but some assumptions include 1) women are more likely to have dry skin, 2) they are more likely to seek a product to cure this condition, 3) the viewer is able to understand the comparison of dry skin to tree bark.

7. "Dry" and "Fix" both fall within the trunk of the tree, and the words are set off by the tree's dark background. The text reinforces the image. At the bottom of the photo, there is more text that explains the function of the product. Viewers may wonder, however, exactly what Curel is promising. For example, the text claims that Curel "locks in more moisture"—more moisture than what? More than not having lotion at all? And because it "locks" in this moisture, it will by extension "heal dry skin better"—again, better than what? Notice that the lotion itself does not heal the skin. Rather, it is its action of locking in moisture that will heal the skin. For more information on "weasel words" such as the ones employed in this ad, see the essay by Charles Lutz in Chapter 1: Advertising and Consumerism.

EDITORIAL CARTOON: BACK TO SCHOOL SALE

1. The cliché in this cartoon is the idea of back to school shopping, an expected precursor to the return to the classroom. The unexpected element that plays off of the cliché is the merchandise "on sale" – bulletproof vests.

2. This cartoon employs dark humor. Few parents would find it funny, but would understand the point the cartoon is making. The harsh reality is that the growing number of shootings in American schools concerns many parents.

3. The cartoon assumes that its audience is familiar with the escalating trend of school violence—at Jonesboro, Columbine, and Santana high

schools, as well as with more local acts of violence with children settling personal disputes and grudges with guns brought to school.

4. The cartoon isn't really "about" gun control. It is rather a social commentary on a trend. One could assume that the cartoonist is for gun control, but then again, he could also be advocating for better security measures in school.

EDITORIAL CARTOON: I HATE THEM

1. It is ambiguous exactly whom the first child hates, and he is the only individual in the cartoon that knows exactly who "they" hate. In the context of September 11, 2001, we may infer that the child hates the people responsible for the terrorist attacks, or by extension, Muslims. He could be feeding off of comments made by his parents, but how precise these comments are is uncertain. However, the cartoon does not necessarily need the context of September 11 to be effective.

2. The second child's comments are highly significant to the message of the cartoon. His statement represents the dynamics of group thinking, and hammers home the idea that hate is an easy concept to buy into. At least he questions the object of the hate; the third child doesn't seem to think it is important. The facial expressions of each child are clearly angry and hard—the final child seems content to simply hate, without concerning herself with the particulars of "who."

3. The cartoonist's claim is that hate is infectious and learned. The first child hates, the second child agrees, although he is uncertain as to whom they hate, and the third child ceases to question. He also demonstrates trickle-down group behavior.

4. This cartoon would be equally effective ten or twenty years ago and ten and twenty years in the future. Hate is timeless, as are group dynamics. Children will still learn hate from their parents and pass the feeling among themselves. The characters may change, but the emotion and dynamic remains depressingly predictable.

NEWS-PHOTO: HOMELESS COUPLE

1. The photographer assumes that the audience will be sensitive to the plight of the homeless, and that they will care about the people in the photo.

2. Some details include the crate the woman is sitting on; the fact that the couple is loitering in an alley on an obviously very cold day, the cup the woman is holding; the many layers of clothing she is wearing (and the coat is out of style, probably a donation to a shelter), and even the couple's facial expressions.

3. Ask students to consider how these elements all contribute to how viewers interpret the photo and presumably the plight of the couple.

4. The couple is not exactly heroic, but not deserving of scorn either. Their faces are almost blank and unreadable. The couple looks certainly downtrodden, but not broken. One wonders if their facial expressions would change if someone came by and put money in the cup.

5. The claim is that homelessness can affect anyone—men and women. Both subjects do not seem to be "typical" stereotypes—they are not dirty, or drunk, or old and unkempt. Their faces still have dignity.

6. The background is necessary to the photo's message. They are in an alley, and they are outside, pushed back from the main path and out into the cold.

7. As mentioned in the answer to question 5, the couple does not seem to fit the cultural stereotype of homeless people. Students may or may not feel that the photo sends a message about urban poverty, or that the photo affects their viewpoint of it.

8. Student responses will vary.

ANCILLARY GRAPHICS

Student responses for this section will vary, but point out how statistical data and factual information featured in these essays could be presented in tables, charts, and graphs.

*Please reference the book's Companion Website, **Dialogues on the Web**, at (www.ablongman.com/goshgarian) for additional class activities and questions, topical resources, links to research and reference pages, online writing labs, and updates to links listed in the book. Also see its "Instructor Resources" section providing teaching, writing, and research links.*

CHAPTER NINE
RESEARCHING ARGUMENTS: THINKING LIKE AN INVESTIGATOR

There are no questions that need to be answered in this chapter for the Instructor's Manual.

CHAPTER TEN
ADVERTISING AND CONSUMERISM

HOOKING THE CONSUMER

TARGETING A NEW WORLD

1. The way advertisers speak about consumers is quite revealing and these three opening quotes effectively emphasize Turow's claims that individuals are "packaged"; that there is a "subscriber base" which includes some and excludes others; and that ratings of an advertisement do not equate to its exposure.

2. Advertisers package or make individuals "useful targets" by separating audiences into different worlds according to distinctions that advertising people feel make the audiences feel secure and comfortable. Students can work in groups to list and discuss examples of "packaging."

3. Turow feels target marketing can result in a "fractured population of self-indulgent, frenetic, and suspicious individuals who will only reach out to people like themselves." Student expressions of agreement or disagreement could revolve around a debate of whether or not they agree with Turow's claim that our nation is "breaking up" and U.S. society is "losing out."

4. The author's tone can be taken as neutral [fact-giving], but it is also one of sincere concern which conveys his disapproval of the extremes to which market segmentation and target marketing dictate consumers' lives.

5. The author fears that target marketing will have far reaching social consequences. "As an entirety...society in the United States will lose

out" (paragraph 16). His primary concern is that if primary medial communities focus on increasingly smaller target groups, other social "categories" will never have the opportunity to learn about the others. Society will become even more economically segregated.

6. Chasing away certain viewers makes the community more pure and more efficient for advertisers; with the irrelevant viewers gone they hope to attract the desirable ones. Exclusion of an audience makes it more economically feasible to tailor materials to small groups/individuals that they know something about already.

BUY THIS 24-YEAR OLD AND GET ALL HIS FRIENDS ABSOLUTELY FREE

1. Kilbourne begins her essay with the statement, "if you're like most people, you think that advertising has no influence on you. This is what advertisers want you to believe." She then proceeds to explain why advertising does indeed have an influence on us, an influence demonstrated by how people react to ads (such as the 1999 Victoria's Secret ad during the Super Bowl). While we may think that media are a means of entertainment and information, to advertisers, "television and radio programs are simply fillers for the space between commercials." Kilbourne provides ample support that advertisers want to influence us, but she fails to prove that they also wish to deliberately deceive us. Ad agencies may argue that people know a commercial when they see it, or that we have the option of not watching or reading an ad if we don't want to.

2. Advertisers know that teens are the most likely demographic to "group think." Quite often, peer leaders set the trends—trends that are promoted by advertisers. The target audience is a group one—get the buy-in of the peer leaders, and you get the whole group. The tactic

preys on teen desperation to fit in, and their insecurities about being part of the group.

3. Kilbourne is clearly troubled by this practice for several reasons. For one, such deals may prevent children from making their own choices. For another, she feels that school shouldn't be a marketplace for sale. She also believes that some of the products touted by these deals are promoting unhealthy choices—such as Coke machines.

4. Many women's magazines feature cooking sections and decadent recipes interspersed with cigarette ads and weight loss programs. Class discussion could also address how commercials on television send women mixed messages. For example, female characters on soap opera programs are rarely featured doing any domestic chores—rather they lead glamorous and exciting lives. Yet many commercials feature cleaning and child care items—items not seen in the make-believe yet desirable world of the soap opera.

5. The example of the Gwich'in tribe in Alaska demonstrates how, in a very short amount of time (10 years), teens were so attracted to television, and the marketing culture it brought with it, that their very culture was at stake. It is an effective example demonstrating how influential advertising can be. Students should discuss the parallels between the tribe and American pop culture and how this example provides a snapshot into our own consumer habits and the influence of advertising.

FRIENDLY PERSUASION: THE GROWING UBIQUITY OF ADVERTISING

1. Student answers will vary but some examples that may encourage discussion is the use of sexy images to sell products, or the implication that using a product will promote social acceptance or happiness. For

example, many diet cola ads feature young and beautiful women. The ads appeal to our inherent love of physical beauty, and our inner desire to possess such beauty ourselves.

2. Fraim provides examples of the "ubiquity of advertising" in entertainment and journalism. Students may also discuss how advertising has infiltrated video games. For example, the NHL 2002 video game by one popular video game maker includes advertising boards surrounding the virtual hockey rink—just like real rinks (another example of the ubiquity of advertising.) And fashion logos, such as Tommy Hilfiger, turn us all into walking ads.

3. This number may seem excessive at first. Ask students to meticulously record how many ads they see from the moment they wake up in the morning to the moment they go to sleep at night. If they wake up to a radio program, they should include the ads; if they wear clothing with logos, they should include these symbols as ads as well. Remind students that ads lurk in many different forms, from trademarks, to commercials, to product placement in games, videos, and television programs. Students may be surprised to see just how many ads they see and hear during the course of a day.

4. Student answers will vary but class discussion may address the way journalists endorse products under the guise of objective journalism. Kilbourne might argue that this shift is already more pervasive than Fraim suspects. In her article, she describes writers who were told to change their stories so that their "reporting" did not offend or alienate advertisers. This shift should make us carefully consider the outside influences that affect what journalists write and the objectivity of what we read.

5. A transaction fee is a business model of online commerce introduced with the emergence of the Internet. According to Fraim, they are the

"new online version of direct marketing." Such fees allow a much broader scope of people to get in on the marketing game.

6.   Student answers will vary. However, Fraim connects his conclusion back to his introduction with his reference of "that door-to-door salesman" mentioned in his second paragraph. His final paragraph may seem out of context. In what ways does this final comment reveal the opinions of the author?

HEY KIDS, BUY THIS!

1.   The anecdote focuses on how the brand-name onslaught literally begins from the moment of birth. The authors emphasize their point by listing the numerous companies who have a vested interest in establishing brand-name loyalty, first with parents, and soon after, with their children. The authors go on to point out that this trend will only escalate as Alyssa may be clothed in "miniature professional basketball jerseys," and wear "Sesame Street diapers" throughout infancy. This early immersion in labels and logos will more than likely create a child who, as early as four or five, has distinct opinions about what she wants and needs in terms of consumer products, and will badger her parents until her desires are met.

2.   The article cites several examples of the negative effects on children (and parents) due to brand-name barrage. Clinical psychologist, Mary Pipher, feels that the daily onslaught of ads "creates in children a combination of narcissism, entitlement, and dissatisfaction." Paula Goedert, a parent of two, also comments. To many parents and consumer groups, advertisers/marketers have stepped over the line, creating a backlash that has resulted in the government beginning to regulate advertising aimed at children. Some parents have also made a concerted effort to limit their children's exposure to ads.

3. Most students will probably agree that the manipulation by alcohol and tobacco companies is obvious, and potentially dangerous. The authors again use statistics, "Marlboro is now the brand name of choice for 60% of teen smokers," Joe Camel is recognized by "90% of 10-17 year olds," and "9-11 year-old children were more apt to recognize the Budweiser frogs…than Tony the Tiger" to point out how companies have insinuated their brands into children's awareness.

4. Despite some evidence of a "backlash against the constant marketing assault facing kids," the authors feel that "none of those efforts, however, is likely to deflect the massive sales machine now directed at children." The authors argue that as long as children have money, they will be targets and that parents must protect their children from the media barrage that encourages uncritical consumer behavior.

THE QUEST FOR STUFF

TWO CHEERS FOR CONSUMERISM

1. Student answers will vary but ask students to consider the reasons why Americans culturally seem to shun materialism outwardly, but embrace it so wholeheartedly as proven by our consumer habits. What is "bad" about materialism? When we say someone is "materialistic," what do we mean? How would Twitchell respond to someone calling him "materialistic?"

2. In paragraph three, Twitchell notes "much of our current refusal to consider the liberating role of consumption is the result of who has been doing the describing" of the role of consumerism in American culture. The "readers" of the commercial "text" are primarily from the fields of academia. Advertising is not considered "high culture" and therefore not worthy of our intellectual attention. For Twitchell, the

liberating nature of consumerism is quite simple: "We like having stuff."

3. Academia does not, overall, embrace the study of consumerism as a legitimate line of inquiry. Twitchell approaches the study of consumerism with humor. He admits that consumerism has, in effect, beaten him into accepting it—his students can quote more jingles than lines of poetry. He also feels that the significant role of consumerism in our daily lives makes it worthy of legitimate cultural study.

4. Critics of advertising assert that consumerism creates a sense of competition and need that leads to greed. The idea of "keeping up with the Joneses" stems from the idea that consumers drive the needs and wants of their communities and demographic groups. Advertising helps push this process along by initiating the *idea* of needing and wanting a product.

5. Objects often hold meaning for the consumer. They may confer a sense of status, belonging, success, or inclusion. While this may seem obvious for items such as luxury items, expensive cars, and status clothing lines, it often holds true for everyday items as well. For example, with the exception of packaging, a lavender soap from the boutique Crabtree and Evelyn is probably of similar quality to a Yardley of London soap on the supermarket shelf. It is the meaning consumers attach to the product that dictates their purchasing habits. Ask students to consider why they chose to wear particular clothing lines or why they buy one kind of spaghetti sauce or laundry detergent over another. While some students may respond that it was the cheapest choice, others may admit it is the brand their mother used or that they were influenced by advertising promises.

MANUFACTURING DESIRE

1. Historically, Americans have viewed "decadence" as excessive indulgence. Prudence, patience, and practicality were celebrated personality traits. Common sense and sacrifice were noble virtues, even among the wealthy. Modern America demands instant gratification; a credit card culture that demonstrates a "celebration of universal human appetites, fully expressed."

2. Versailles-era France and Imperial Rome are both times known for their opulence and Flood's point is that contemporary America is similar as a place of mature decadence—decadence that has "grown systematic in its excess." A discussion about what happened to both of these "empires"—namely a tremendous and devastating fall may help students consider the connection between decadence and possible disaster.

3. This example supports the author's points because this Toronto woman believes $37,000 is not enough of a salary for her family to live on. Her remark about this as living life "in poverty" remarks on the hyperinflation of the concept of the word "enough," further supporting Flood's thesis about America's decadence reaching new heights. Bombarded with media images and advertising celebrating the high life, she feels that she falls short of what she needs—indeed what she *deserves*—to have a comfortable life.

4. Student answers will vary.

5. Student answers will vary.

THE STUFF OF LIFE

1. Sanders notes in paragraph 10, "Whenever I return from a sojourn in the woods...I'm dismayed by the noise and jumble of the workday world. Time in the wild reminds me how much of what I ordinarily do is mere dithering, how much of what I own is mere encumbrance." Sanders feels that consumerism, and the culture it drives, prevents us from seeing and doing the important things. We are a gluttonous and compulsive society, and our consumerism threatens to destroy the planet. A possible response to Twitchell is that while Sanders may concede that we are indeed a consumer driven society, we must learn to say "enough."

2. Early consumerism was driven by convenience. As people centralized power, moved into towns, and developed systems of barter-based commerce, they began to accumulate wealth and demand. The desire to display wealth and prosperity through the accumulation of things has its roots in earliest civilization.

3. Student answers will vary but class discussion may include how government is directly promoting the opposite of what Sanders is advocating. Instead of encouraging restraint, in 2001, the Bush presidency approved a unilateral tax refund. The president encouraged Americans to spend—not save—the refund to "stimulate the economy."

4. Sanders feels that conserving resources is not only good for future generations, but that it would help the current generation lead less frenzied lives. Paragraph 27 outlines his vision for this simplification. Class discussion could address the plausibility of this paragraph. Does consumerism prevent people from doing the things he lists? Would simplifying our lives indeed encourage these behaviors?

5. Student answers will vary.

THE $100 CHRISTMAS

1. Student answers will vary but the class should address the variables involved. For example, $100 divided amongst a family of six would leave each member approximately $16.66 each. Is this sum then divided by five to give a gift to each family member? The equation is quite different for a family of three or two. There are no rules or restrictions on the request—perhaps the family can decide to buy a family gift, such as a DVD player. The class should also discuss the principles involved in the minister's request, and whether they believe in such principles.

2. Student answers will vary but students may discuss how the "spirit of giving" seems to be confused with the spirit of greed. When you consider how stores bring out Christmas and Hanukkah decorations in October, and children's Christmas advertising kicks in around August, McKibben may have a point.

3. Television, which serves as a vehicle for advertising (see Fraim's article earlier in this chapter), bombards children with clothing, food, toys, and trips, creating a sense of need and want that taps into children's desire for fun. Sophie has been sheltered from this onslaught so she really doesn't know what she is missing.

    An interesting issue to address in class is the quality of life between children today and children from 20, 50, even 100 years ago. Did children of the 1970s, or 1930s enjoy childhood any less? Did they feel deprived? It isn't until the child is able to evaluate options—in this case, options delivered by television—that he or she is able to formulate desires.

4. The holidays of Christmas and Hanukkah are religious celebrations. By encouraging their members to reject the commercialization of these holidays, they are indeed trying to "stick to religion." The columnist seems to have forgotten why people celebrated these holidays in the first place.

THE LANGUAGE OF ADVERTISING

WITH THESE WORDS I CAN SELL YOU ANYTHING

1. Most copywriters would not agree with Lutz's contention that advertisements are written to trick the customers. Although thy may admit to tapping into popular consciousness it is likely that most would instead argue that the words used in the ads are those that most people are familiar with and respond to positively. The connotations of these words are universally understood, according to those who write the copy for the ads.

2. A product is considered new for a period of six months during a national advertising campaign, and for as long as two years if a product is being advertised in a limited test market. A product is also considered new if it has undergone "a material functional change." This does not have to be an actual improvement in the product; just a simple alteration will qualify it. Thus, it is easy to side step the regulatory intention by creating a "new" product by adding lemon scent, for instance. In other words, product performance does not have to be improved. These regulations seem to assist efforts of advertisers to mislead the consumer. Consumers should identify exactly what is "new" before buying a product.

3. Student answers will vary.

4. The author uses an informal, chatty, humorous tone throughout the article. Many comments are not only informative and instructive, but also quite entertaining. See the ends of paragraphs 18 and 19, for example. He engages the reader very directly in the process of analyzing weasel words, giving his reader instructions if not commands in order to get them involved.

5. Some readers would prefer that the essay ended at paragraph 50. The parody seems an odd and awkward tack-on. First the theme of the poem, "the power of advertising to meet our needs and solve our problems," is not directly relevant to the preceding discussion of weasel words. Although humorous, why end with a poem about advertising in general when the essay deals with a very specific subject—weasel words? In straining to be funny and entertaining, students may feel that Lutz made a poor choice for a conclusion.

6. If a manufacturer makes up a trade name for its product, then advertises that only this particular manufacturer has the product, the technique could be considered circular reasoning. For instance, the Goodyear ad, "If it doesn't say Goodyear, it can't be polyglas," is really saying, "If it doesn't say Goodyear, it can't be Goodyear's (polyglas) fiberglass-reinforced tire."

THE LANGUAGE OF ADVERTISING

1. Open for discussion. Many students will recall the efforts of many groups to have the Joe Camel banned. Students can debate over whether outlawing is an effective solution.

2. O'Neill says that writers "must glamorize the superficial differences" when product differences do not exist, or they must create differences by getting the audience involved in the action in the ad, not the product

itself. Ask students to share examples of current glamorized advertisements that involve the audience.

3. O'Neill cites seven charges that have been made against advertising. In support of advertising, O'Neill's primary argument is simply that advertising language is only a reflection of the society around it, and that "slaying the messenger would not alter the fact—if it is a fact—that 'America will be the death of English.'" Furthermore, he says that advertising does not *force* us to buy anything, but rather stimulates the development of new products in the marketplace and conveys certain information. Anticipating the objections lends support to his claims since his rebuttals are logical; students may even note that these are already mainstream beliefs.

4. Any number of symbols may be suggested. O'Neill refers to the use of the color red in the depiction of autumn and fire to suggest warmth, experience, and wisdom. Other symbols could include the strong-armed man on the Mr. Clean detergent bottle. O'Neill believes repeated exposure of such symbols acquire the power to call up in the consumer's mind a host of ideas and images that could not be communicated as effectively in any other way.

5. O'Neill's style could be described as "advertising" style. In his own writing, he makes use of some of the techniques he describes. First, he personalized his writing, involving the reader in the communication process. Several times in the introduction he addresses the reader as *you*. To emphasize his point about the simplicity of of language, he supports his narrative with the most effective kind of testimonial available, an invitation for the reader to conduct fog index calculations on ads. Furthermore, O'Neill's own language is simple and direct. In a sense, he is selling the language of advertising in his discussion, without raising his vocabulary or voice. Finally, he carefully engineers his own

language to mirror the practices of ad writers by carefully selecting the words.

6. Student answers will vary.

THE SELLING OF REBELLION

1. & 2. Since these questions are closely related, begin by referring to paragraph 7 with its description of the relationship between rebellion and American society. Student opinions will vary as to whether the connection Leo makes is a valid one, but discussion will likely address the notion that America was founded upon such ideals of rebellion. Historically, America has espoused ideals of freedom and, to a certain extent, rebellion. Ask students to make a list of historical events that they could say are based on the rebellious spirit of an individual or group.

3. Again, baby-boomers date back to the 1950s and 1960s, so the previous discussion could be extended to when this particular group of American society was raised. In evaluating who advertisers target and what desires they target, ask students to review the products mentioned in paragraphs 4-6 and/or to bring in their own examples to determine whether such a connection between the theme of breaking rules and this generation exists. While it may be the case with cars, what about perfumes, etc.?

4. Define modernism and postmodernism for students so that they can have a basic understanding of the chaotic tendencies of postmodernism, e.g. that one does not refer to a single meta-narrative, therefore, there is a continual questioning of authority and no supreme rules to break. Students will likely agree that pop culture and the "anything goes" or "everything is shown" media ignite the flame under such relativistic behavior in advertisements.

50

5. Open for discussion but remind students of Leo's opening statement that television advertisements like the one for Isuzu are "some of the worst cultural propaganda." Could exposure to such advertisements lead to dangerous behavior with products that promote breaking rules?

*Please reference the book's Companion Website, **Dialogues on the Web**, at (www.ablongman.com/goshgarian) for additional class activities and questions, topical resources, links to research and reference pages, online writing labs, and updates to links listed in the book. Also see its "Instructor Resources" section providing teaching, writing, and research links.*

CHAPTER ELEVEN
GENDER ISSUES

GENDER AND SELF PERCEPTION

SAPLINGS IN THE STORM

1. Pipher uses this analogy to emphasize her claim that adolescent girls in America become vulnerable and eventually "lost" as they conform to cultural perceptions. Have students locate places in the text where Pipher employs this analogy and discuss the before and during adolescent behavior of girls. Ask students to think of times when they too have lost or pushed aside their "authentic selves" due to cultural pressures and then ask them to share how they "resurfaced."

2. Student answers may vary, but direct them to the three factors Pipher states "make young women vulnerable." If students do think girls must make sacrifices to socially fit in, have them elaborate on *what* is sacrificed and *how* that sacrifice leads to peer acceptance.

3. Pipher feels "androgynous adults are the most well adjusted." Have students make separate lists of the behaviors androgynous girls and boys would benefit from to highlight their prescribed notions of gender roles; note the differences and ask how the transition from adolescence to adulthood might further change these and why.

4. One way of having students see if Pipher's article is of universal application is for them to isolate one paragraph and replace the word "girls" with "boys." In thinking of parent-child relationships and corporate America's influence, the gender of an adolescent might not matter, but what issues that Pipher brings up are solely in relation to girls? Have students debate the issue of perceptions and images to note any differences in opinion that are gender-based.

5. Have students first define the intended audience of this piece. If it does not include men, ask them what parts of the piece could be considered general concerns for adolescents, then speculate on what Pipher's *male* clients' issues might be. If she had included some adolescent male issues, how would her thesis be different? Return to question number one and ask students to consider if and how adolescent *boys* "disappear mysteriously into the Bermuda Triangle."

6. Lead students through brief descriptions of gender stereotypes of the 1930s, 1950s, etc., noting national concerns of the time periods. Ask students to note Pipher's examples of Michelle, Holly and Gail and then to place these three girls' problems into the different historical contexts. Discuss how the underlying social pressures facing these girls have changed according to each decade and how Pipher's advice to them might change also.

WILL BOYS BE BOYS?

1. Leo states that "teachers know that girls are better suited to schooling." The problem is, he doesn't say *which* teachers, what grade they teach, in what sort of school system, or any other circumstances that may or may not influence such a broad assertion. Leo discounts many other factors—children's temperament, home life, social experience, etc. One could argue that there are many well-behaved or quiet boys, and equally rambunctious girls. His support is shaky—he refers consistently to an ambiguous "they" throughout the article. The effect gets his readers on board, and may even stimulate their ire, but some teachers and parents may disagree with him due to his lack of solid evidence.

2. Leo seems concerned that boys are getting the short end of the stick—socially and intellectually—in American schools. He feels that educational facilities, driven by "feminist agendas" are "pathologizing" typical boy behavior. His conclusion of "save the males" summarizes his overall point.

3. Again, Leo provides very shaky evidence without clear references to actual people and circumstances. For example, he links the trend of the "case against boys" as occurring in the "wake of the feminist movement" implying that it is *caused* by this movement. The logic is faulty, especially without solid evidence. His comment about "sexual harassment" also has no support—he may have a case, but without the actual circumstances, he seems just to be riling the crowd.

4. Student answers will vary but discussion may address how his solutions would actually work in practice. Moreover, would his solutions solve the problems he outlines in paragraph 9?

BUMP AND GRIND: LITTLE GIRLS STRUT THEIR STUFF

1. Student answers will vary but class discussion can address what these costumes are meant to mirror and why? What would these outfits look like on young women? What does the song to which the child dances and lip-syncs glorify? And do "sexualized" clothes mean the same thing on a child that they do on an adult?

2. Parents who may have allowed their children to dress in the way Rodell disapproves may fear that she is right and must defend their choices. Or they may object to the idea that young children can be viewed in any other way than young children. Or, they may simply see no harm in the "sexualized consumer culture" to which Rodell objects.

3. Student answers will vary.

4. Rodell identifies "they" as the girls and women who embrace sexualized consumerism. Like Leo, Rodell's "they" is faceless and ambiguous. However, "they" seem to be highly influential and supported by popular culture—a tough force to fight.

THE BULLY IN THE MIRROR

1. Alexander has an epiphany while looking in the mirror in his hotel room while he is on vacation with his parents. He realizes that his size and shape prevent people from wanting to get to know the "real" him. His reaction may seem abrupt and drastic. Students may disagree with how drastic, however. He could have dieted and pursued lighter athletics for example. Other students may applaud his efforts to take control of his body. Alexander himself clearly feels he made the right choice, but Hall seems to indicate that Alexander is driven by cultural pressure rather than by healthy lifestyle choices.

2. It is ironic that Alexander has substituted one body image for another, and neither is the "real" him. He clearly prefers one over the other, but his efforts are masking a deeper issue—that as a society, we are unwilling to accept people for who they are on the inside.

3. Student answers will vary, but discussion can address how images of heroes and action figures influence boy's behavior and image of the ideal male figure.

4. Cultural messages include the glorification of muscular figures--such as of wresters and action heroes, pressure to athletically outperform peers, and the attraction of shortcuts. Children see exaggerated body images every day, in toys, video games, and cartoons. The influence may be subtle, but pervasive.

5. The author refers to many experts and medical specialists in his essay, including Drs. Harrison Pope and Roberto Olivardia. He traces Alexander's personal experience, cites studies, and interviews teens. His support provides solid evidence for his conclusions and balances his essay as a well researched piece.

GENDER COMMUNICATIONS

NO DETAIL TOO SMALL FOR GIRLS ANSWERING A SIMPLE QUESTION

1. Student answers may be influenced by gender—a fact that can be explored in class. Males may feel that some (much) of the information females relate is unimportant, while females may place more importance on the body of information conveyed. There does seem to be some truth in Kornheiser's assessment that women and men convey and interpret information differently, but not that one "dispenses it without discrimination."

2. John Leo may find this response interesting (see "Will Boys Be Boys?"). Perhaps because women feel that mathematics skills are more valued in our society than communication skills, it is necessary to defend the idea that girls are good at math too. Or that because a majority of power is still held by males, they are jumping to defend girls to balance this power. Class discussion could address if this stereotype hurts girls or not.

3. Kornheiser says that he prefers male communication styles. However, his essay is very exploratory and reflective—traits that he seems to attribute to female communication.

STOPPING FOR DIRECTIONS (CARTOON)

1. Student answers will vary but the class may split up along male/female lines to explore this question.

2. Women may feel more comfortable asking for directions because culturally they are "allowed" to be vulnerable. Men are not afforded this consideration—culturally they are supposed to be self-reliant and independent.

3. Many authors would probably agree that there could be a genetic link as well as a cultural one.

4. Student answers will vary but class discussion should address the cultural aspects of this stereotype. If the stereotype does not cross cultures, then the "genetic programming" is called into question. If something is genetic, it should cross cultures and ideologies to be more or less universally true.

I'M SORRY, I WON'T APOLOGIZE

1. Student answers will vary, but also have them think of examples of their own when an apology was not given. Was it due to the pride of one's gender?

2. America's tendency to not apologize is one that may or may not lead to cultural resistance since America is the leading world power. However, the tendency to not apologize could have significant effects *within* America. Tannen points out in paragraph eleven that many people imprisoned for crimes never say that they are sorry, which allows for conjecture that such individuals could become repeat offenders. No contrition equals increased crime rates. Besides

58

criminals, American society as a whole would increasingly become less democratic and more self-centered due to the lack of "I'm sorry's."

3. Many of the points Tannen makes are applicable to the Clinton apology. Take for instance her remark in paragraph twelve, "Apologies seem to come most easily from those who know their error was unintentional." Students could debate over whether his affair and subsequent cover-up was intentional.

4. Student answers will vary.

5. Thinking about Segal's quote will lead students to contemplate the term "unconditional love." Segal seems to be saying that if people love each other unconditionally, then they will automatically forgive everything—but is this really the case in relationships between friends, family members, and spouses? Tannen's revision of the phrase might be more realistic by today's standards, so student's responses may evoke such attitudes.

IN EACH OTHER'S COMPANY

1. Once students have made such lists, have them collaborate in groups to revise lists (add items and re-word others) and then present them to each other to compare and discuss the basis for the lists—socialization or biology. Since socialization factors will most likely be the foundation of their lists, try to elicit what biological factors could bring about "obvious differences" between friendships?

2. Consider why readers are given the detail that Bill is a concert promoter. Does this mean he relies on communication more than Gold's other friends? Throughout the entire essay there is a juxtaposition of action versus communication. This could be a reason why Gold makes his request, and if women's friendships are

considered less physically active, the likelihood of them making such a pact is lessened. However, remind students that this latter point is of Gold's making and not a universal thread of female friendships.

3. Gold's support is primarily based on personal anecdotes and his credibility as a published interviewee on "male bonding." He also focuses on a select group of men—divorced fathers. This limits his views on relationships as it suggests men only have friends with other men when they do not have women in their lives. To dispute Gold's limited views, students may reflect upon the male-male, male-female, and/or female-female friendships they have had throughout their lives in school for who they have "bonded" with most closely to note if gender consciously or unconsciously affected such bonds.

4. Besides the "un-male" action of kissing fellow male friends, it seems Gold is more upset by the fact that his friend did not understand his points about self-love. Gold also accuses his friend of getting caught up in the "politically correct feminist notion," which he feels is not relevant to their discussion of male friendships.

5. Again, this question refers to the action versus communication aspect of male-male friendships. Students should return to the adjectives they noted as they read to determine why a male author would make such a statement. If racquetball is a test of physical endurance, how it is also a builder of male friendships?

THE COMFORT OF FRIENDS

1. Throughout her essay, Quindlen notes that her female friendships are based in verbal communication, which is "probing and intimate" while men's are "skin deep" (paragraph three). Have students discuss their opinions regarding verbal communication in their friendships and then direct them to Quindlen's final sentence, "We talk, therefore I am."

Have they ever experienced the fulfillment Quindlen has by talking to their friends and did the gender of the friend(s) make a difference?

2. Student answers will vary.

3. Quindlen's reference to a "man's-woman" classifies women who see other women as competition for men, but students might also consider this term to describe women who are like men in that they exhibit strong competitive natures in all pursuits.

4. Students may find that because she talks and depends on talking to this circle of friends that Quindlen's friends are similar, but point out to them that each provides "a sympathetic ear" from a different perspective and/or frequency. Such a close analysis of the circle of friends will also evoke some of John Gray's ideas about Mars and Venus in that Quindlen's friends do not offer directions or immediate suggestions for improvement.

5. Again, these comparisons highlight Quindlen's claim of the importance of talking to learn about yourself and your world. In terms of playground behavior for girls, *conversation* is a contact sport. This is something Quindlen now sees in her daughter's life and hopes for her son.

6. The "sad" aspect of men's friendships to Quindlen's friend is that their emotional and professional lives (or what they perceive these lives *should* be) would never let them drop everything to comfort a friend diagnosed with a sickness, nor would they "laugh, cry and talk and talk and talk" together for a whole weekend. The traditional view is that men are not nurturers or sensitive enough to console someone in such a situation, again returning to the thesis that men's friendships are skin deep and not based in verbal communication (even Herbert Gold half-heartedly remarks, "Talk may not be as true as racquetball, but

discussion can sometimes arrive at understanding"). Have students debate the issue.

FEMINISM IN THE 21ST CENTURY

THE INDEPENDENT WOMAN AND OTHER LIES

1. Discussion of the title of Roiphe's piece can begin by having students identify the words that connote a "lie," which should lead them to paragraph 2 and the word "façade." Answering "Why" such words and ideas are "lies" will require students to consider if they can accept the ironies and contradictions that Roiphe discusses, such as the "refined version of the double standard."

2. Guide students through the paragraphs that cite examples and critique each one on its effectiveness as support to her claim. Ask them to consider the fact that most of her examples are either of friends of hers or pop theorists on the issue. Are these reliable sources? Why or why not? This can lead into a debate on the universality of the issue.

3. Explaining the term "rape fantasy" may raise students' eyebrows, but its use as an analogy does parallel the "man in the gray flannel suit" as both configure women desiring men in power positions over them.

4. Student answers will vary.

5. Student answers will vary.

IN THE COMBAT ZONE

1. Have students seek Silko's answers to these questions, but extend the discussion to ask them for their personal answers to them as well. Do they agree or disagree with Silko's claims?

2. Student answers will vary. If the majority disagree with Silko's father's comment, asking them what they feel could equalize the differences between men and women.

3. Defining patriarchy can stem from a discussion of gender role stereotypes. What are "traditional" male and female roles? A discussion of what feminism is should also supplement remarks on patriarchy. How does the issue of one gender assuming it has more power transfer into physical acts of violence? Remind students to focus on violence from strangers toward women, not domestic violence.

4. Have students reflect on each of the five rapists described in terms of power. How could they scale them in such terms, i.e., which do they think had the most desire for power and why?

5. Students can explore what their feelings are about women who can defend themselves and why these two male groups might fear such women in their lives. With respect to the application of this statement to American society, have students define what American belief systems in terms of what gender relations are. Then consider what the differences would be for women living in rural and urban regions of the country. Silko gives examples of potential acts of violence upon her in both settings.

6. First ask students what they understand Silko's thesis to be. Ask students what the main point of this example is to see what support it offers to that thesis, then ask them to consider how the essay might read if this example was deleted.

7. Considering all of the examples Silko offers to justify women's use of firearms, guide students through the metaphors she creates, e.g. who/what is hunted and by whom?

REVISIONIST FEMINISM: A DIALOGUE

1. Faludi takes the offensive—she expresses concern that the discussion will be unproductive because of the type of "feminists" (which she sarcastically puts in quotes) aren't the sort of people who listen to other points of view. One can see how Lehrman would respond to this tone and onslaught of criticism—an onslaught that precedes any discussion on the topic itself—by initiating defensive measures, such as mentioning Faludi's condescending tone. Ask students for their opinion in beginning a "dialogue" in this way. Does it prevent discussion, or get to the point?

2. Faludi feels that true feminism differs from the propaganda spread in the 1970's about feminism. Feminism didn't "fail" she explains, consumer culture's promises about feminism did. In paragraph 8, she states her view "Feminism is and always has been about women acting in the world as full-fledged citizens, as real participants in the world of ideas and policy and history…. It's about insisting on the right of women to dignity, a living wage, meaningful work, and active engagement in the public arena…. Feminism, real feminism, is about freeing women to be genuine individuals—and recognizing that such individuality doesn't come in one size only or out of a bottle."

3. Lehrman feels that the more radical left feminists, like Faludi, make it difficult for other women, who do not embrace all their political and social values, to disagree with them. She fears that women who make choices that are not "feminist" according to women like Faludi, will not be respected by the feminist status quo. Lehrman is advocating that true feminism is the freedom for women to make choices—even

64

choices that might not appeal to women like Faludi. In paragraph 4, Lehrman comments, "…all women don't think alike, and as far as feminism is concerned, they certainly don't have to. The only items on the real feminist agenda are equal rights and opportunities, a society capable of accepting the widest array of women's choices, and women strong and independent enough to make rational ones." Paragraph 13 reiterates this point.

4. Student answers may vary but compare the two definitions of feminism provided by each woman in questions 2&3. Both seem to agree that respect and freedom to make choices are fundamental to feminism. Both agree that feminism is often a victim of the media, and misunderstood by the general population because of media slanting.

*Please reference the book's Companion Website, **Dialogues on the Web**, at (www.ablongman.com/goshgarian) for additional class activities and questions, topical resources, links to research and reference pages, online writing labs, and updates to links listed in the book. Also see its "Instructor Resources" section providing teaching, writing, and research links.*

CHAPTER TWELVE
SEPTEMBER 11, 2001

A DAY OF INFAMY

THIS IS WHAT A DAY MEANS

1. September 11, 2001 changed our perception of safety and security on our home soil. We went from a "state of innocence" to a state of shock. We considered American soil to be set apart from the strife of the rest of the world, a feeling reinforced by the fact that we are physically separated by oceans from much of the world. Sullivan explains that this sense of safety has been violated in a way we never expected—on an ordinary workday, on a beautiful September morning.

2. Normalcy relies on the expected, on routine. In paragraph 2, Sullivan notes that while normalcy is not the same thing as freedom, it is quietly dependent on it. American freedom is built upon principles of "life, liberty, and the pursuit of happiness." Fundamental to these principles is that normalcy prevails—we expect certain circumstances to be routine—it is safe to go to work, to fly, to dwell in cities; our government is secure, our values are protected, and our property and persons are safe from attack. Without normalcy, such basic freedoms would be difficult, if not impossible, to protect.

3. In paragraph 5, Sullivan describes the symbolism of the United States to us and to other countries. In paragraph 11 and 12, he describes and explores how this idea is held sacred.

4. Student answers will vary.

LETTER FROM GROUND ZERO

1. Student answers will vary, but class discussion could address the way different generations feel about war. The class could also address how

previous conflicts in the middle eat color our perceptions of who terrorists are and are not.

2. Students may need to research this moment in history before formulating their responses. Similarities include the unexpected nature of the attack, the fact that it happened on American soil, and our loss of security at home. Differences include that Pearl Harbor happened during wartime, had fewer casualties, was a military target, and was "official" – one country was attacking another. Discussion may also address how American response is similar and/or different from Pearl Harbor, and why.

3. As Schell describes in paragraph 8, he feels that "annihilation" is a very real threat to the world. He advocates a worldwide ban on weapons of mass destruction, an end to the Middle East's festering conflicts, and a "politics of globalization" such as that described by Britain's Prime Minister Tony Blair.

4. Schell connects escalating unrest in the Middle East, and a conflict of values at work. Students may wish to discuss *why* terrorists from the Middle East view the United States as a target.

WE CHOSE HONOR

1. Weisel says that unexplained murder is cowardly. It would take courage—or be more "daring"—for the terrorists to stand up and explain their actions and choices. He also feels that terrorism is senseless violence, as he describes in paragraphs 5 and 9.

2. Weisel defines evil in paragraph 9: "Hatred is at the root of evil everywhere.... For those who glorify hatred, as terrorists do, the end justifies all means, including the most despicable ones."

3. Instead of reacting to terrorism with chaos and fear, American found instead a sense of unity and common purpose. Paragraphs 10, 13, and

14 describe how this unity was manifested—in government, by selfless acts of courage, by outpourings of support and caring. Weisel's title reflects his view: America acted with bravery and honor, rather than fear and cowardice.

4. Student answers will vary.

CARTOON: UNCLE SAM

1. Dressed in what looks to be a stripped down fire fighter's uniform, Uncle Sam is depicted as a rescue worker, sleeves rolled up. His mouth is slightly agape, as if he cannot fathom the amount of work to be done, or the level of devastation he sees. His crossed suspenders—which center the eye directly on him—reinforce this image of labor and effort.

2. The Empire State Building remains standing, a symbol of modern progress and an icon for New York City. Through smoke and rubble, New York still stands.

3. The woman represents "every victim." An innocent. Women tend to project more vulnerability. The effect would not be as strong if Uncle Sam was carrying a man.

4. Uncle Sam has traditionally represented American government and war recruitment. He is a symbol of war, fighting, and justice. The phrase "Uncle Sam wants you...to join the US Army" may also apply here---Uncle Sam carries an innocent victim of an act of war on U.S. soil. Students may discuss why or if this figure is more effective than others, such as the Statue of Liberty.

5. Student answers will vary.

PATRIOTISM AND THE FLAG

TRUE TEST OF PATRIOTISM IS HARDER THAN JUST WAVING A FLAG

1. Student answers will vary.

2. Kane feels that much of the flag waving after the September 11 attack was inspired by a knee-jerk response to the situation. It was a popular thing to do. He also notes how some "flag-waving yahoos" were also in turn terrorizing people who they felt didn't look American. Students may discuss if such people harm the image of the flag or create the negative feelings about the flag and the people who display it described by Kane and some other authors in this section.

3. Student answers will vary, but Kane seems to be outwardly supportive of Bush or of the government in general. He may assume similar feelings from his audience.

4. Student answers will vary, but discussion can address just how far journalistic impartiality must go. Is wearing a flag on one's lapel a political statement? Would Kane feel the same way about an Italian reporter wearing an Italian flag? Or if a journalist wears a breast cancer ribbon does it mean he or she supports one charitable cause over another? Are journalists barred from having political leanings? Why or why not?

THE WAY WE LIVE NOW

1. According to Packer, the flag represented for many liberals a government they disagreed with and a war they were against. This mentality from the 1960s and 70s continued for many of them to the present. Separation between conservatives and liberals meant that liberals—even "pro-American" ones—did not display the flag out of concern that they would be associated with the political right.

September 11 flag displays conveyed a message that transcended politics and protest—we (Americans) were *all* attacked, we are one nation, a community, and the flag links us all in common.

2. For Packer's parents, and by natural extension, Packer himself, the flag was associated with the undereducated, blue-collar, conservative working class (good ol' boys). Student answers may vary but class discussion may address whether such distinctions existed in their own communities and whether they remained after September 11.

3. Packer relates the story of the man who killed a Sikh (not a Muslim) in Arizona and an example of how some people twist patriotism into an excuse to incite violence.

4. Packer assumes that readers will understand his point of view. He assumes, for example, that readers will likewise understand why his parents would never have a corduroy sofa, and how this distaste for such an item translates into a deeper ideology. Other assumptions include familiarity with the network "Comedy Central" or the political vibe on college campuses.

5. The author's parents clearly influenced his adult viewpoint. As a child, the author enjoyed playing war games and the excitement of make-believe combat. As he describes in paragraphs 2, 3 and 4, his parents felt that displays of patriotism were "simple bad taste." This viewpoint has caused him some anxiety about displaying the flag now. He is inspired by the flags he sees, but he still hasn't gone out and bought one himself.

RALLY ROUND THE FLAG

1. The two authors would perhaps agree with how flag waving is more of a fashion statement and political bandwagoning rather than a display a true patriotism. But Kaufman is more flexible in his viewpoint, he sees

the other side of the display, and admits that he loves the flag. But like the other authors in this section, he also harbors some reservations.

2. Paragraphs 7, 8, and 10 describe some of the feelings Kaufman has regarding the flag and the love/concern relationship he has with it.

3. Kaufman prefers the more peaceful "This Land is My Land" to the more aggressive "God Bless America." Students should discuss how the songs are similar and different, and which they prefer and why.

PHOTO: BOX OF FLAGS

1. Student answers will vary.

2. Student answers will vary.

3. Student answers will vary, but class discussion may address how photos support the text they accompany and the importance of context to understanding what we see. Is it necessary to know the context of this photo? Why or why not?

4. Student answers will vary.

REACTING TO TERRORISM

AMERICANS DON'T UNDERSTAND THAT THEIR HERITAGE IS ITSELF A THREAT

1. America represents a value system and a way of life that the terrorists resent and fear. Their attack of "symbols" of the American system—of commerce and government—is the "rational" demonstration of their objection to this lifestyle, political and economic system.

2. Carr explains in paragraph 12, that the terrorists fear a death of their own value system and their way of life. They are witnessing an erosion of their own cultures, and view America as the source of this erosion. "Inside those buildings, the people behind this attack believe, is where the end of the societies they come from and the values that they live by was and is being planned…and *there* is where the erosion must be stopped."

3. We have had several wars of values on American soil—the British attack in 1814 is one Carr closely connects to terrorist motives today. Our Civil War was likewise a war on a value system and way of life. Carr warns us that wars of this type are not easily ended. "What our enemies want is nothing short of an end to our predominance, and they will not forsake terrorism until either they attain that result or we make such behavior prohibitively, horrifyingly expensive."

4. Student answers will vary.

THE ALGEBRA OF INFINITE JUSTICE

1. Roy prepared this essay for a British newspaper. Because this audience was more removed from the events of September 11, they could be more apathetic to the situation. They also live in a country where criticism of America is far more commonplace then it is in the U.S. Roy's tone is sarcastic and even contemptuous, and she makes sweeping assessments of America and Americans that may work well for her British and Indian readership.

2. Roy makes broad assumptions in this essay, many of which are not supported by actual evidence or facts. For example, she repeatedly implies that America is quick to anger and to blindly find a scapegoat. In fact, the U.S. government proceeded with far more caution than even American's expected. Again, Roy may be tapping into her audience's commonly held assumptions about America.

3. Student answers will vary but her description of America is of a huge bully easily angered, quick to fight, and slow to think about the consequences of its actions.

4. Roy's argument is that the American government should carefully consider the reasons behind the attack, and address those reasons, rather than to immediately punish the perpetrators. Terrorism is a symptom of a larger problem, but not the actual problem itself. Until the problems are addressed, no successful reduction of terrorism can possibly happen.

5. Paragraph 13 offers a vague solution. Connecting back to question 4, Roy would like to impress upon U.S. leaders that they must admit culpability in causing the anger that motivated the attacks. She also fears that the U.S. will violently retaliate (she notes Japan's attack on Pearl Harbor and the subsequent, albeit some time later, result of Hiroshima). Leaders are unlikely to respond to her views because they go counter to the American way of life they support and protect. While British readers may be able to see her viewpoint, many U.S. government leaders are unlikely to do so.

6. Student answers will vary.

UNDERSTANDING TERRORISM: A HARVARD UNIVERSITY ROUNTABLE

1. A definition of terrorism, as demonstrated by the Harvard professors, clearly does not have a simple answer. However, they seem to agree that terrorism is fundamentally political in nature. It is violent, and it is symbolic. The victim of the terrorism is not the audience. Rather, the victim conveys a message to the audience. Finally, terrorism is an act committed against innocents, or, non-combatants. It aims to carry a message through the attack of innocent people. And because innocent people are the targets, terrorist actions are shocking and therefore get

more attention. For several professors, terrorism is a technique; the *means* defines terrorism rather than the goal.

2. Innocents are better defined as "non-combatants." As Stern explains, all terrorists feel that their cause is justifiable. Victims are therefore, to the terrorists, a means to defend or support this cause. A troubling issue is whether terrorism is ever justified. Does it boil down to simply whose side you are on?

3. Stern comments that terrorism is a moral issue because it goes against the mandates of international law and religious tradition. She objects to the technique used, the methods of terrorism, rather than the reasons behind the action. Terrorizing an innocent group of people, killing them in the name of a cause, is morally wrong. Even our response to terrorism has moral ramifications—we must retaliate in a morally responsible way, or be as culpable as the terrorists are.

4. Bush faces multiple issues, including simply defining the task. Carter suggests developing "Homeland Security" as he describes in paragraphs 39-40. America has enjoyed a certain isolation from conflict, now our own soil is at risk. Stern adds that Bush must seek vulnerabilities in the terrorist network, no easy task considering the terrain and the support they may have in the countries they inhabit.

5. Fundamental to the connection between the Middle East and acts of terrorism is a long-festering anger against the West, and most of all, the United States. There is a general hostility and anger in the Arab/Muslim world against the US. The US is seen as the leaders of a globalization that threatens their way of life and leaves them politically powerless. Paragraph 57 details more of this resentment. This mass anger can build and feed terrorist acts, and even create a sense of support for those people who act on this anger. Paragraph 61 addresses the cleansing value of violence. "Even random violence against a perceived oppressor is seen as a redemptive act." And in this case, the U.S. is viewed as the oppressor.

6. Advice comes on two levels: for the government and for the people. And unfortunately, the advice is not particularly comforting. First, Americans must look beyond the act of terrorism and understand its motivation. They must also be aware that catastrophe is possible—weapons of mass destruction in the wrong hands could have devastating consequences. There is little doubt that members of Al Qaeda would use such weapons if they had them. Americans must look for sabotage. Yet, in light of all this danger, Americans must also keep risk in perspective. Finally, listening to and even heeding international opinion will have an important role in addressing the issues behind terrorism in the future.

7. Student answers will vary.

*Please reference the book's Companion Website, **Dialogues on the Web**, at (www.ablongman.com/goshgarian) for additional class activities and questions, topical resources, links to research and reference pages, online writing labs, and updates to links listed in the book. Also see its "Instructor Resources" section providing teaching, writing, and research links.*

CHAPTER THIRTEEN
RACE AND ETHNICITY

STEREOTYPES: HOW THEY HURT

FAMILIAR STRANGERS

1. "We" are the people he identifies in his first paragraphs "Latinos, Hispanics, Spanish." "You" are the white "Anglos" who wield economic and political power. The audience can really be both these groups. Although the "you" implies that the audience is the white reader, educated Hispanic readers are clearly identified as the topic of discussion and would embrace many of his points. Suarez's use of these pronouns emphasizes the division between the two groups.

2. Suarez notes that unlike other immigrant groups who come across oceans, Hispanics have the "Old Country two hours away by jet…[which] means these new Americans don't have to slam the door on their place of origin." Hispanics are therefore able to maintain stronger cultural ties than other groups.

3. Student answers will vary, but class discussion can address how both statements are true and false, and why.

4. Paragraph 8 describes the ethnicists and what they support.

5. Members of the Hispanic middle-class tie the values of their homes to "Anglo" investment in the area. They wish to retain their Spanish roots, but also desire to compete economically and intellectually with the white status quo. Above all, they desire respect from society in general, and hope to serve as role models for Hispanic youth.

THE MYTH OF THE LATINA WOMAN: I JUST MET A GIRL NAMED MARIA

1. Feeling like an "other" is universal, but Ortiz Cofer's argument offers sound examples of the differences between Puerto Rican and "white" cultures. Most evident are the ones that revolve around fashion, but direct students to her statement in paragraph 1, "Oh that British control. How I coveted it" which hints at a difference in demeanor. Also, paragraph 4 ends with a comparison between Puerto Rican festivities and American parties.

2. Begin by asking students to determine what America's cultural ideology is and what is considered mainstream. Other than Hispanic cultures, students should consider the problems other cultures may face due to heritage and geographic history.

3. Student answers will vary but ask them to recall movies and music they have seen or heard that portray Latina woman as seductive temptresses. Have they seen anything in the media that has *not* offered that image?

4. The island system of morality centered life around family and religion, predominantly Catholicism. These customs liberated young girls to feel free to wear what they wanted to show off and celebrate the bodies God gave them, but then restrained them as their over-protective brothers made sure to limit the responses to such provocative displays (paragraph 6). This leads to misunderstandings when the island culture is removed to a foreign and less understanding environment that holds different ideological values.

5. Ortiz Cofer's poem at the end of her essay reinforces her claim that while different races/cultures with different customs do speak to each

other, they have not fully realized that their languages are not exactly the same.

6. As "one of the lucky ones" Ortiz Cofer attributes her fortune to her family's incentive to allow her to advance her education and travel. Ask students if they feel this statement excludes Puerto Ricans who will never have a "public life," and if so, do they feel Ortiz Cofer's points to be weakened. Has she denied her culture in any way by calling herself a "lucky one"?

ONE OF THE BAD GUYS?

1. Hanania's response was one of confusion and anger. He learned that Arabs are "bad guys" and that Hollywood, government, and security view them suspiciously. This attitude trickles down into daily dealings of his life.

2. Paragraph 5 details the "Arab look." Simply because he looks like the bad guys in the movies—dark and swarthy—he is followed in airports and his activities tracked by the government. His only provocation—he looks the part.

3. Student answers will vary, but mention in class discussion that this essay was an opinion piece in Newsweek. How do you think the events of September 11 would influence Hanania's essay today?

4. Hanania, perhaps surprisingly, is not asking Hollywood to stop portraying Arabs as "bad guys." Rather, he wants equal billing—if you are going to show the bad, show the good too. But Hollywood is based on stereotypical depictions of people, and for now, Arabs fit the stereotype.

WHO IS A WHIZ KID?

1. Thinking about editor's jobs as ones that try to exclude bias, Gup was probably surprised that this supposed neutral voice was using a classificatory "them." The quote also suggests Asian Americans have been excluded from reportage thus far.

2. As the evidence in his article suggests, reactions from parents and teachers may be different as they may place a burden on children to succeed in areas not natural to them. Stereotypes that Gup mentions also prove the divisions among races today. Ask students to think about how these races could converse with one another without preconceived notions about each other.

3. Gup claims individuality is denied when stereotypes are assumed as reality. They become representative of the race rather than people seeing individuals as products of their parents' influences and personal commitment (paragraph 6).

4. Ask students first to discuss what they know about inner city conflicts and then try to come to an agreement or disagreement with Gup's comment.

5. Offer students an overview of Hitler's viewpoints regarding the power of the German race and the wars and horror it lead to all over Europe. Although students may not recognize the myth to be active today, discuss the prejudices, if any, Jews face today.

6. Student answers will vary.

ASSIMILATION

THE RETURN OF THE MELTING POT

1. The more liberal culture of America these days accepts and seems to advocate diversity and individuality as a means to success and this is what Schlesinger supports with his revision to the national currency slogan "e pluribus unum."

2. Student answers will vary, but construct debates for and against the idea of a group self-esteem.

3. Responses can return to the "*e pluribus unum*" reference as America paradoxically considers itself a unified place of freedom and democracy. Schlesinger's use of the example emphasizing the importance of Irish Americans assimilating into mainstream culture agrees with his argument that a culture first ingest its own and then explore, rather than argue its way in to the mainstream via "turgid" facts.

4. Schlesinger supports this statement by going beyond the historical events of immigrants first moving here to explain a current society that does demonstrate its own experiences. Direct students to paragraph 18 where "Western democratic tradition in its true proportions" is described because it reminds us that when Europeans first settled here, they did not know what the proportions were.

5. Student answers will vary but have them share experiences with each other in class discussion.

FORGING A NEW VISION OF AMERICA'S MELTING POT

1. For James, the "idea of America" apparently did not include immigrants. However, the "idea" is indeed influenced by immigrants—by their expectations and hopes, and by their successes. While the idea of a "melting pot" may seem appropriate, it implies that immigrants blend into an existing social order. Multiculturalism, the buzzword of the last decade, rejects this melting pot and the concept of assimilation.

2. Mexicans represent the biggest immigration group in the United States today. Notes Rodriguez "As such, they are the most likely to leave a permanent imprint on our culture." Class discussion may include some of the ways this has already happened, and how it may continue.

3. Student answers will vary but comment on the similarities between Suarez's use of "we" and "you" and Rodriguez's "us" and "them." The two authors hold similar ideals, but different perspectives.

4. Paragraph 10 explains how Mexican America's tradition of mixed ancestry is likely to continue in the United States as more immigrant populations marry within the existing population.

5. Mexican Americans are more likely to intermarry. They are less likely to view mixed ancestry as taboo, and their identity is more fluid. They already wield some political clout, and adhere to a much looser definition of "ethnic infrastructure." Paragraph 20 further details how romantic views of mixed ancestry will further encourage cultural synthesis. Mexican Americans won't just blend in; they will influence cultural change as they "assimilate."

DIVERSITY AND ITS DISCONTENTS

1. It seems Madrid's examples of locations like Peru and Pakistan are
    exotic because one does not hear of them everyday—not as many
    immigrants have come from those countries. And although Madrid is
    an American without immediate family in exotic locations, he still
    classifies himself as "other" because of his name, physical appearance,
    and speech patterns (paragraph 2).

2. In paragraph 5 Madrid states, "School was where one became
    American." In school, ideas of uniformity as acceptance pervaded
    through socialization and discipline, and it is likely school
    administrators and teachers unconsciously created this myth with the
    goal of creating a school that ran smoothly. It is a myth for the same
    reason Madrid refers to himself as "other"--appearance plays a more
    significant role in acceptance.

3. Unlike "academic protectionism" which considers curriculum for
    students, "intellectual protectionism" refers to the hiring and
    subsequent treatment of professional academics in a university.
    Ethnicity should not be an issue, but it is and Madrid brings up this
    aspect of the multicultural education debate. The impact on students
    would be that respected professors from varied cultural backgrounds
    could be seen as role models to students of all races and backgrounds as
    well as educators offering new perspectives to their field of study.

4. Americans of a city and not a village atmosphere are undeniably
    different, which is what the pastor is pointing out to Madrid's
    grandmother. Ask students if they find this story disturbing
    considering the idea that such non-acceptance would happen in a place
    of religious worship. Also, the fact that the pastor warns Madrid's

grandmother of such a possibility suggests that such behavior may have already happened.

5 & 6. Both questions ask students to reflect upon Madrid's definitions of these words and can be taken as an opportunity for group work. Students can discuss Madrid's definitions and grapple for meaning with each other in order to advance their own.

7. Student answers will vary.

PLEASE ASK ME WHO, NOT "WHAT" I AM

1. Student answers will vary.

2. Student answers will vary.

3. In paragraph 10, Lite describes an incident she viewed on TV in which a "pack of white boys beat, then chased a terrified black teen onto a highway, where he was struck and killed." This episode, she explains, "silenced" her.

4. People respond in different ways, but many describe their own ethnic backgrounds. Lite believes that some of these people hope that her own ethnic diversity will help her understand their own. Others, she believes, simply want to categorize her.

5. Student answers will vary.

RACIAL PROFILING

YOU CAN'T JUDGE A CROOK BY HIS COLOR

1. Racial profiling maintains that people of certain races are more likely to commit certain crimes. As such, it is inherently racist in its assumptions and in its practice. However, all races are subject to profiling. A white man walking around in a prominently black neighborhood may be profiled by the police as out of place and more likely to commit a crime. A woman acting suspiciously in a department store may be watched more closely for possible shoplifting than a man would be. The question arises, therefore, if everyone is subject to some form of profiling, is it still racist?

2. Student answers will vary, but it may seem that the foundation of Kennedy's argument is that racial profiling is morally objectionable. He concedes that it works, but that it is unjustifiable because it also hurts innocent people. If something is morally wrong, can it have exceptions? Moral objections tend to be absolute.

3. Paragraph 18 presents two examples that are not truly connected to crime, and therefore may not serve as particularly effective examples. Ask students to come up with better examples. Bryonn Bain's essay later in this section may provide more tangible examples of why racial profiling is harmful.

4. Kennedy's solutions include spending more money, increasing the number of police officers, and stopping more whites so that they will know how racial profiling feels. Kennedy's use of the word "simply" trivializes the very real budget issues faced by many police departments across the country. It is a fairly well established fact that law enforcement budgets are traditionally low. Implementing the

changes Kennedy proposes means that police would need more money, which would raise taxes. It is not a simple issue and his lack of acknowledgement of the complexity of the problem may leave holes in his essay which opponents could use to disassemble his argument.

5. Both authors include this comment to show that even blacks, who are subject to racial profiling, will profile along the same lines as law enforcement. Kennedy maintains that the practice is still wrong.

6. Racial profiling increases minority distrust in the criminal justice system, which can in turn influence how juries determine cases. They may be more likely, for example, to free a guilty person because they feel that the way the person was caught committing a crime was inherently unjust.

IN DEFENSE OF RACIAL PROFILING

1. Derbyshire traces the history of the term "racial profiling" while explaining that the practice is much older than the phrase itself. The issue entered the political arena as a debate item around 2000. This historical tracing may support his contention that political rhetoric is driving the controversy rather than the practice itself.

2. Politicians publicized the issue, created the catch phrase, and increased public awareness as a positioning piece. By making it a political issue on which a politician must assume a position, the public likewise must determine where they stand on the issue.

3. Student answers will vary, but the fact that Parks is a black law enforcement official may carry more significance.

4. Derbyshire notes that since 2000, it is pretty much political suicide to officially approve of racial profiling or even admit that it is used. In paragraph 10, he notes that it is particularly dangerous to admit, citing the case of Carl Williams who was fired the day after he discussed the issue. Derbyshire implies that the practice continues, even with the support of the Supreme Court, but that law officials are silent on the subject for their own safety.

5. Derbyshire's position is that racial profiling is justified because it is supported by statistical fact and is therefore a useful tool for law enforcement in the fight against crime. Student answers will vary on whether Derbyshire's position has merit.

6. In paragraphs 31 & 32, Derbyshire explains that racial hysteria creates an atmosphere in which one group of people fear that another is "filled with malice" toward them. "…As long as we continue to pander to that poisonous, preposterous belief, we shall only wander off deeper into a wilderness of division…"

CARTOON: RACIAL PROFILING

1. The scene is set at the National Archives in Washington D.C. where an African American man and his son look at the Bill of Rights. This document ensures freedoms and protections of all citizens. The man holds a newspaper under his arm that explains the reason for his statement.

2. Bennett's political stance is obviously against racial profiling. Racial profiling denies the basic rights outlined in the Bill of Rights. Bennett wishes to send a message to his audience through his art.

3. As an editorial cartoon, it most likely appeared in editorial pages of newspapers or in a news-journal.

4. Most of the authors in this section would agree with the sarcasm expressed by the man in the cartoon. Derbyshire may agree with the premise behind the cartoon, but not that racial profiling should be stopped.

THE BILL OF RIGHTS FOR BLACK MEN: WALKING WHILE BLACK

1. Bain is trying to connect the rights assured to all people under the Bill of Rights to the injustice of his experience and how it violated this document. His articles, outlined using the same formula as the Bill of Rights, reinforce this image. Student answers will vary on the effectiveness of this technique.

2. Student answers will vary.

3. By emphasizing certain words, he is able to demonstrate the force of the words, the harshness of the words, and the humiliation of the words. He highlights an attitude of the speaker. As readers, we are indignant at his treatment, insulted by the police officer's words, and sympathetic to Bain's plight.

HAILING WHILE BLACK

1. Student answers will vary.

2. The "elephant in the living room" is an expression used to describe a situation in which people try to pretend things are normal when there

really is an enormous unspoken issue that they must get around. For Steele, this elephant is the fact that black crime is statistically higher than white crime. In discussions that involve race, we can pretend that this statistic does not exist, but until it is directly addressed, we are simply skirting issues.

3. As he explains in paragraph 4, racial profiling is less of an issue than a coded argument "over how much racism exists in society today." Racial profiling is a new political buzzword associated with the "black experience." It touches on multiple issues connected to race, justice, and fair treatment under the law and by society.

4. Student answers will vary, but Steele himself muses on how he would have reacted. Even the fact that he did indeed catch the first cab symbolized something to him, a fact that troubles him.

*Please reference the book's Companion Website, **Dialogues on the Web**, at (www.ablongman.com/goshgarian) for additional class activities and questions, topical resources, links to research and reference pages, online writing labs, and updates to links listed in the book. Also see its "Instructor Resources" section providing teaching, writing, and research links.*

CHAPTER FOURTEEN
WHAT MAKES A FAMILY

RETHINKING THE NUCLEAR FAMILY

THE NEW NOSTALGIA

1. An ideology is a system of interlocking beliefs and values; the gender roles Barnett and Rivers present here will probably look pretty familiar to students. Women are expected to stay home, care for children, and set aside careers so they can spend time bonding with children. But men are harmed as well. They are unprepared for emotional intimacy with their wives and children, and can't assume a practical role in daily child rearing activities. They are supposed to be tough, even boorish. The authors scoff at the "warrior within" school of thought as an overcorrecting, silly return to exaggerated postures of masculinity. Barnett and Rivers don't say that men have actually become weak"; in fact, they connect such qualities to a fullness of human character that transcends stifling macho roles.

2. Barnett and Rivers disagree that change is dangerous, abnormal, and unhealthy—in general, it's normal, healthy. The images these authors use are especially effective in deflating the idea that change is a monster. Women "juggle the demands of work and home," like frantic sideshow acts; politicians use guerrilla warfare's extreme "slash-and-burn macho tactics" to get by; media is "keeping the bonfire going" (a witch-hunt? Bonfire of the vanities?); the present is "bumpy," but on closer inspection the bumps are not mountains; the past was "a golden age" of "lofty perfection"—language usually reserved for myth. Even some of the literal descriptions can be funny—e.g., the legislators, aides, and university scholars described in paragraphs 18-19 seem to be a bunch of old duds caught in a time-loop.

3. The 1950s weren't that great, at least for most women. A woman stayed at home trying to keep up a cheery facade for her family; despite her hard work, mothers were then blamed by social critics for "smothering" their children. Men actually had it pretty good, if the abstract satisfaction of working to support the family was enough. But their children remember these men as "distant and overly-involved in work," so there were some trade-offs. We've adopted this model of family as ideal because it was enshrined in the first well-developed sitcoms broadcast for national consumption, and entrenched in cable channels specializing in syndicated reruns of these shows.

4. The authors believe that the same forces that created the model two-earner family are working to shape a family stronger than the falsely idealized one of the 1950s. A flattened job market will not allow men and women to attain a bloated sense of self-worth through work, or even to survive on one partner's paycheck. Thus men and women will cleave to each other for emotional fulfillment and financial viability. We're already seeing some signs of this trend, since people are marrying and having children later; the next step is a lower divorce rate. Students might agree that tighter marriages and lower divorce rates are desirable, and indeed are happening. However, they might disagree with the reasons the authors give, explaining the trend by a return to old-time values and moral fiber. Or, they may disagree with the conclusions, since the authors haven't supplied any statistical evidence to prove that what they say is really happening.

5. Barnett and Rivers distrust the media as a collective cry-wolf dismissal of the strengths and successes of the contemporary American family. It is imperative that they show how media distorts our impressions of family if they are to argue successfully that we're better off than we think. In paragraphs 20 and 21, they observe that news media don't accurately "mirror" who we are—they don't provide an accurate, full reflection. Instead, they "frame" what they want us to see, leaving out

92

important information about past rates of violence and abuse in order to make daily headlines more gripping. Political reportage calls gentle, thoughtful politicians "wimps." Movies aimed at young men titillate with blood-lust, but hardly provide an accurate portrayal of what masculinity really means. Likewise, 1950s sitcoms succeeded by showing us pictures of unattainable bubble-worlds, which engage us by their sheer swerve away from lived reality. The authors want readers to understand that we are confused because we've taken these flashing projections as truth rather than as entertainment.

WHAT'S HAPPENING TO MARRIAGE?

1. The authors contend that the institution of marriage—which locates its origins as a vehicle to promote the social order of family and economic stability—is more of a life choice for couples. Divorce has diluted the expectations of the institution itself. Moreover, some people view marriage as an outdated institution with its roots in the subjugation of women and religious/political conservatism.

2. Student answers will vary but it is likely that many will agree that it is a choice between couples (much as the authors describe).

3. Fifty percent of all marriages end in divorce. This fact may influence some couples to simply give up on unfulfilling relationships. Divorce has also created an "easy out." Finally, if marriage itself is not seen as an absolute lifetime commitment, some people may be more cavalier about getting married knowing that if it doesn't work out, they can simply move on.

4. Student answers will vary but the argument can be made that social taboos of premarital sex are not as strong as they used to be. Few couples are compelled to marry for sexual reasons alone.

5. Paragraph 12 details how the expectations and attitudes of young women influence the institution of marriage as a social force. Women are more pessimistic about the longevity of marriage. They are more tolerant of children born out of wedlock. And they have higher expectations of the men they marry. They expect equitable sharing of housework and childrearing. They are economically independent, and less likely to put up with unfulfilling relationships.

6. Paragraph 20 describes how the institution of marriage is likely to continue to weaken but the authors are still hopeful that the next generation will seek out more stable relationships. Students should discuss what their expectations of marriage are as they represent this next generation the author's describe.

WORKING DADS, UNITE!

1. Achenbach's tone is sarcastic, although students might remark how sincere some of his comments seem at first glance. Particular statements that stand out include: "What's more, men are now expected to help raise their children as though they were their own," and "If we have to spend all our time at home raising kids, then we have to spend more time at work doing the serious goofing off that we used to do at home." Readers know that he is joking, but humor often masks personal, unspoken issues and hidden truths.

2. Spending too much time with a parent is not healthy, especially with a parent who is dealing with stressful work situations. Working parents are always trying to achieve a healthy balance between the amount of time and energy they spend on their work and at home, and Achenbach's argument seems to be that fathers are under more pressure because of their prescribed role as breadwinners. Students may wish to discuss if this role is self-imposed, or a social reality for working families.

3. America's capitalist society defines success in terms of financial earnings. Therefore, work done outside the home is considered more valuable. What this quote brings up, and what Achenbach fails to address, is the issue of mothers in the workplace and stay-at-home fathers. Ask students why they think Achenbach did this and how his argument would change if he considered this perspective.

4. Achenbach thinks that the 4/3 solution is "meant to shame people into working fewer hours while not placing the entire guilt trip on working mothers." His impression of researchers in general is also humorous because he feels that they don't live in the real world.

5. Since this essay originally appeared in GQ magazine, his audience is primarily male. This is further evidenced by his use of the collective "we" as a substitute for "men" and "fathers." Readers of other magazines may see the humor of the piece, but it may not be as effective because its overriding thesis is directed toward promoting solidarity among working fathers.

SINGLE MOTHERS, MENACE TO SOCIETY?

1. In paragraph 10, Coontz describes the stories of "three ... never-married mothers" who differ in class, educational status, and age. Students can dispute whether these three stories are enough to prove Coontz's point: that it is unfair to generalize about the morality of all single mothers. The point that "there are hundreds of paths leading to single motherhood" (paragraph 9) is central to Coontz's essay because she wants to argue that the morality of any individual unwed mother's case is much more complicated than people like Alter will admit. Given that some stories "would seem irresponsible to even the most ardent proponent of women's rights," and "others stem from complicated accidents or miscalculations that even the most radical right-winger

would probably forgive" (paragraph 9), Coontz believes no one can condemn all single mothers collectively.

2. Aside from the moral claim that no one person should pass judgment on single mothers collectively, the major claim of this essay is that innocent children will suffer from recent attempts to stigmatize illegitimacy. One of the most important strategies Coontz uses to make this point is by creating a vivid picture of her son Kristopher. Far from being a pariah, Kristopher emerges as a typical American adolescent. By practicing "his electric guitar" at apparently astonishing volume, Kristopher is behaving like middle-class American teenagers everywhere; because he seems so typical, readers can well imagine that, like most adolescents, he "takes labels very seriously" (paragraph 4) and is sensitive to being branded as illegitimate.

   Both this sensitivity, as well as a certain principled self-confidence, is conveyed when Coontz describes Kristopher standing up to a teacher who made a "particularly cruel remark ... about single mothers" (paragraph 5). Coontz evokes Kris's self-confidence again when she worries that it "might lead him to do risky things or to question authority once too often" (paragraph 15). Kristopher emerges, then, as a child who seems to have suffered little in self-confidence from being the son of a never-wed mother. Furthermore, society seems to have accepted Coontz because she is educated and respected.

3. In paragraph 8, Coontz offers several examples of how attacks on illegitimacy seem motivated by a desire to return women to traditional roles. Coontz also cites an article which suggests that social problems would be solved if women allowed themselves once again to be "'cared for' by men." Later, Coontz argues that "[the new family-values crusade also appeals to those uncomfortable with the changing role of women by emphatically reestablishing men as the "heads of households..."" (paragraph 17). She describes with derision President

Clinton's remark that children of unwed mothers…aren't sure they're the most important person in the world to anybody…(paragraph 18), a comment Coontz claims reflects centuries-old attitudes which denigrated women's role in child-bearing and child-rearing.

4. Coontz uses ironic, sometimes sharply connotative language to describe her opposition in paragraph 1. Her description of politicians and pundits "going on about the dire consequences of single parenthood" suggests the talk is so much meaningless, repetitive drivel. The ominous adjective "dire" is ironic in its overstatement. Similarly ironic is the word "menace." The verb "trumpeting" conveys her derision of writers by subtly comparing them with pack animals ("of every stripe"). Coontz ends the paragraph with language which insists on her own humanity, in comparison with these pack-like creatures: such "mean-spirited and cynical" invective "takes my breath away."

5. In a canny response to "family-value" conservatives, Coontz hearkens back 300 years to Native American tradition. In response to European Jesuit missionaries who encourage the Montagnais-Naskapi Indians to "take control of women's sexuality" and "discipline their children more harshly," the Native Americans respond with what sounds like a magnanimous sense of community and parenthood: "You French people love only your own children ... but we love all the children of the tribe..." (paragraph 19). By identifying her point of view as the oldest one within a multicultural understanding of the word American, Coontz establishes herself as the traditionalist, a position almost always taken by those who attack illegitimacy.

WHY I STILL THINK I'M RIGHT

1. Quayle is advocating that traditional family structures are still preferable to non-traditional ones. He believes that children are best reared in a two-parent household "with a mother and a father." This is

an opinion piece, and Quayle provides little support as to why this is the best structure; he simply feels that he is right.

2. Quayle cites time pressure—time spent on "computers, on the phone, in the car and at the mall" as the root of family turmoil and dysfunction. He also identifies "economic pressure" caused by a materialistic society, and pop culture that "tears down" the institutions that give us stability. Ask students to consider the validity of this list and whether they agree with all or parts of it.

3. The fact that Quayle is "heartened" by the fact that single fathers are raising children does seem a bit hypocritical in light of his criticism of single motherhood. However, he does add that he hopes that both parents would remain committed to the care of the child.

GAY MARRIAGE AND PARTNERING

VIRTUALLY NORMAL

1. The basis of this concern is the conservative view that "homosexual life…is worse than heterosexual life." Sullivan addresses this claim by reminding readers that homosexuals already belong to heterosexual families. As he points out in paragraph 5, it is the heterosexual familial rejection of homosexuals that destroys families. Have students discuss which perspective they support and why.

2. Student answers will vary.

3. To illustrate Sullivan's use of "they" when speaking of the conservatives, refer to the following statement in paragraph 3: "They mean by all this 'the other,' against which any norm has to be defended and any cohesive society protected." This terminology persuades the reader to consider the conservatives "the other" instead of

homosexuals. Therefore, something is not right/normal with the way "they" are thinking and arguing against homosexual marriages.

4. The reasons for homosexual depravity include familial rejection. By including both views of the issue, Sullivan uses the argument of depravity to prove that the conservative views beg the question. Students can discuss whether they found this identification of fallacies a strengthening point of his essay. After examining Sullivan's points they may also try to find fallacies that weaken his own argument.

5. Hadley Arkes' claim, in sum, is that men need women. Sullivan uses Arkes' argument to discuss the option of heterosexuals remaining single. If they can remain bachelors, why can't homosexuals; and conversely, if men need to marry another for care and support, why can't that person be a man? In discussing Sullivan's evaluation of Arkes, direct students to paragraph 8 and the argument about what is "socially preferred," marriage or bachelorhood? Also ask students if they think Arkes was really advocating "feminizing society." The need of a female influence in a man's life is not the same thing as feminizing society.

6. Waverers are single people who waver on the decision of marriage. The only options are to marry or remain single. In terms of gay marriages, conservatives refuse to embrace virtuous homosexual men, but for wavering women, a lesbian relationship is socially preferable. These views are all based on Arkes' argument about the necessary presence of women.

7. Open to discussion. Have students describe the qualities of both audiences. Is one more liberal than another? Or is there a large majority of college students who are equally conservative?

WHO SAYS BANNING GAY MARRIAGE IS IMMORAL?

1. Students might not be convinced that Jacoby's argument is based on conservative principles because the socially damaging movements he cites, such as Apartheid, are reduced to mere disagreements. His problem with banning gay marriage in moral terms is that he doesn't feel you should deem an immoral act moral just because more people than not tolerate it: "It is an argument against the pretense that same-sex marriage is required as a matter of decency."

2. The *New Republic* is a magazine that addresses political, social, and economic issues in the United States. Andrew Sullivan happens to be a senior editor of this publication. Ask students to go online to www.thenewrepublic.com and read some of the articles there. Jacoby highlights this magazine because of its political and social slant, and to demonstrate how another forum of opinion has "cast the issue [of gay marriage] in explicitly moral terms" when he feels that "morality does not clamor for a change."

3. Student answers will vary.

4. To counter the position that gay marriages are not "natural," Sullivan stays away from sexuality entirely. Rather than focusing on marriage's function to legitimize sexual expression, he focuses on marriage as a hallmark and a prerogative of citizens, and as an emotional commitment. To counter the objection that some religions might find gay marriage unacceptable, he brings out the war-club of separation of church and state; you can't object to this principle and remain a patriotic American. Further, he points out that gay marriage leaves completely untouched the question of whether churches would need to change; churches retain their autonomy. Jacoby may respond to these points with his primary comment—he isn't against gay relationships, it is just that marriage is an institution that creates a union between a

man and a woman. As such, it simply isn't appropriate for same-sex couples.

CARTOON: FAMILY VALUES

1. Student answers will vary.

2. Student answers will vary.

3. Wasserman's cartoon portrays a well-dressed, clean cut gay couple as a loving, hand-holding relationship who calmly request what they feel they are entitled to—a marriage and a mortgage. Their political opponent is portrayed as an aging, overweight overreacting homophobic, who reacts with panic. Through his art, Wasserman is clearly supporting the gay cause.

SAME SEX MARRIAGE

1. Essig "couches" her responses in the "subjunctive." She doesn't want to disappoint her friends and family, and she doesn't want to appear as if she disapproves of their life choices. But she doesn't agree with the general principle of marriage, which she doesn't see as a union of souls, but an outmoded institution designed to oppress women.

2. Essig's tone is a bit antagonizing. She is critical of marriage and while she says that she supports other people's right to do what they wish, she also comments that she will not celebrate the marriages of other lesbian couples who do make this choice—further proof of her disapproval.

3. Student answers will vary, but students should compare her responses to the points outlined by Jacoby in the preceding essay.

4. Student answers will vary, but ask students to comment on how Sullivan addresses this issue—how would he respond to her assertions?

WHAT'S LOVE GOT TO DO WITH IT?

1. Student answers will vary, but it is interesting to note that Graff was skeptical about marriage herself at first, before she found herself "stumbling onto something sacred."

2. "Holy Matrimony" was a weapon used by the Protestant movement to make a case against Catholic celibacy. Marriage became a sacred union of souls. As such, two people should have a spiritual as well as a physical connection. In other words, they should love each other. This led to the radical idea that marriage was a union of spirits, and youth should therefore have a say in who they married and why.

3. Although the shift began in the 18th century, it was during the Victorian era that this transition became most apparent. Courtship practices involving the active participation of both young people became the norm. The car enabled courtship to become more intimate and out of sight of parents.

4. This question is best addressed by encouraging class discussion about how youth culture influences courtship rituals. The car, for example, enabled youth to expand their geographic region of courtship, provided a private place to conduct courtship, and supplied the means of escape from parental control and scrutiny. Ask students to consider how courtship has changed from their parents, and grandparent's

generations, and how much of this shift can be attributed to youthful rebellion.

*Please reference the book's Companion Website, **Dialogues on the Web**, at (www.ablongman.com/goshgarian) for additional class activities and questions, topical resources, links to research and reference pages, online writing labs, and updates to links listed in the book. Also see its "Instructor Resources" section providing teaching, writing, and research links.*

CHAPTER FIFTEEN
CASEBOOK: JUVENILE CRIME, ADULT PUNISHMENT?

ADULT CRIME, ADULT TIME

1. Open for discussion, but direct students to sections such as paragraph 5 for definitions of the two terms. If a delinquent is a neglected or rebellious child whose actions are those of a truant, vandal or petty thief, what constitutes a "criminal"? With regard to the justice system, however, more is made of the difference between children and criminals than of delinquents and criminals.

2. Refer to the history provided in paragraph 8. Compare this information with what students already know. Their thoughts on the juvenile system may stem from the operating principle Collier mentions.

3. Collier does not offer a solution to the shortcomings of *guardian ad litem*. The connection between her explanation of this system and her argument is that it proves juveniles who have not committed serious crimes are not helped by a coddling system; therefore, more criminal justice intervention is needed for those who do commit adult crimes.

4. Megan's law requires that advance notification be given to a neighborhood when a convicted sexual predator re-enters their community. Although it is unclear whether Jesse Timmendequas was a juvenile criminal, the "national outrage" and eventual legislation that was passed proves, and thereby supports, Collier's argument. If people voice their opinions loud enough, change *can* happen. She hopes that the same will happen in reaction to Jonesboro or other nationally publicized crimes by juveniles.

YOUNG AND ARRESTLESS

1. Recidivism is the tendency to lapse into a previous pattern of behavior, especially a return to criminal activity. Current juvenile court policies give young criminals a chance for retribution and a clean slate, which makes it hard to determine repeat offenses.

2. Labeling theory is explained in paragraphs 11 and 12. Students can argue for and against its effectiveness and attempt to explain whether a criminal intentionally labels him/herself by committing a crime.

3. Strain theory is detailed in paragraph 10. Its connection to current expungment policies is primarily that it seems dependent on the crimes committed and if a criminal stated reasons for acting in such a way. The percentage of those who commit crimes is assumed, under the strain theory, to be those who have been denied societal advancement. Ask students to discuss who is denied these days—always those in minority positions? Denial could be seen as more universal.

4. Direct students to paragraphs 18 and 20. In sum, expungment interferes with law enforcement because judges will not know of previous offenses and will assign lesser sentences to those they believe to be first-time offenders. Funk argues that society as a whole will suffer expungment practices because judges unknowingly return more career criminals to the streets.

5. Funk's essay structure is inductive in that its opening example sets up the specific problems with the current juvenile criminal justice system. What follows is his general commentary on the issue, how other sources have addressed the issue, and subsequent recommendations. Ask students to rate its effectiveness with the essays read thus far on the same topic.

THE MAXIMUM SECURITY ADOLECENT

1. Talbot's story of Stackhouse effectively draws in the reader by presenting a real case of how zero tolerance laws are causing harm to kids who may not necessarily deserve such harsh treatment. Actual cases are an effective way to engage audiences and make them care about how the factual information supports the case.

2. Talbot intersperses Stackhouse's story with facts about the legal system and the history leading to his present situation. Lenient juvenile laws are being replaced in the wake of school massacres and gang warfare with inflexible adult penalties. Paragraphs 14-19 details the history of the juvenile detention system, and how it has changed over the last 30 years. Her information presented in paragraphs 24-27 presents statistical data and research. Some people may argue that her presentation of the Stackhouse case could be overly sympathetic, and that many teens that commit vicious crimes deserve to be tried as adults, but others may point out that this case is a troubling example of how the system is hurting kids who don't deserve it.

3. Student answers will vary but it does seem unfair that Jeff is deemed an adult, but the other kids involved—who are the same age as he—are deemed children. Would the case be different had the gun been loaded? Or if someone had been killed?

4. Paragraph 24 & 25 discusses how young juvenile offenders "spent much of their time talking to more skilled and experienced offenders who taught them new techniques of committing crime and methods of avoiding detection." Furthermore, 30 percent of teenagers prosecuted in criminal court were rearrested over a period of up to two years, as compared to 19 percent who had gone through the juvenile system.

Such a statistic indicates teens prosecuted as adults are more likely to commit a crime again, exactly what the nineteenth century judge had warned.

5. The Gault case opened up the doors for the criminal courts to start trying juveniles as adults. "If you give kids adult rights, you can give them adult time." The Gault case involved a judge punishing a 15 year old boy for a crank phone call with six years in a juvenile facility. An adult who committed the same crime would have received a maximum sentence of two months or a $50 fine. When the Supreme Court overturned the conviction, it included that the boy's constitutional rights had been violated. The argument follows that if kids have such constitutional rights, as adults do, then they should be held equally accountable for their crimes, as adults are.

6. Student answers will vary but studies indicate that juveniles are more likely to be influenced by older and more experienced adults. They are housed and often jailed with adults and as such they are more vulnerable to sexual exploitation and physical brutalization. Paragraphs 23 and 27 touch on some of the risks unique to the juvenile offender incarcerated in adult prisons.

7. Student responses to this question will vary, but paragraph 27 points out the strange scenario that although a teen may be charged as an adult for a crime, because the teen is still under 18, they "can't get a Tylenol" without a parent's or guardian's permission. If a teen is declared an adult by a criminal court system, shouldn't they be considered adult henceforth?

CRACKDOWN ON KIDS

1. "Zero tolerance" is the idea that to be young is to be suspect. It is becoming the "mantra in public schools and juvenile courts because of the way adults have "criminalized" kids. Fuentes defines the term as punishment for any transgression from drug, alcohol and weapon policies. Students can express their agreement or disagreement with Fuentes' definition and discuss if and how they have heard the term "zero tolerance" used.

2. Fuentes writes of the shift in adult attitudes, which began roughly a generation after the height of political and social movements created by young people of all colors. The reasons she gives as to why public opinion is shifting against children are the lack of family structure and the vilification of youth when their worlds do not coincide with ours.

3. Fuentes contrasts rather petty "juvenile" crimes with serious "adult" crimes, and these examples support her belief that children are not "evil incarnate," rather, they have been criminalized. Whether this juxtaposition helps or undermines her argument is open to discussion. However, by establishing this comparison, readers may be left questioning her argument with a "yes, but..." response.

4. Fuentes does cite many credible sources such as the National Center for Juvenile Justice, the Justice Department, Attorney General Janet Reno and the ACLU, which strengthen her essay. Students can work in groups to isolate other data and examples in order to discuss their effectiveness.

5. Open to discussion. "Dennis the Menace" is a mischievous character—a young child—who cannot help getting into scrapes. But Dennis' antics are presented as innocent childhood goofs—he does not

commit outright crimes. Once again, readers may be left questioning her example, as few people would parallel the actions of Kip Kinkel, Dennis Klebold, or Andy Williams with those of "Dennis the Menace."

6. Student answers will vary.

GUN CONTROL

THE RIGHT TO BEAR ARMS

1. Open for discussion. However, the point may be made that most of these incidents involve unregistered guns, so that Burger's suggestions of tougher regulation of handgun registration would not be effective. Reform in these instances would need to take place on the level of the suppliers of illegal weapons—involving law enforcement authorities rather than lawmakers.

2. Burger does a good job of pointing out how the concerns which necessitated the Second Amendment in the eighteenth century have long since changed. Students can discuss at what point do we consider changing Amendments when they are no longer valid in light of social, intellectual, political and technical advances. The issue comes down to how flexible the Constitution was intended to be: should such a document "change with the times?"

3. Open for discussion, although there is a point where "taking the law into one's own hands" does not constitute a viable defense in court.

4. Student answers will vary. Some students may object to the idea of government control of handgun registration and ownership, while others may feel that even more regulation is necessary. Still others

110

might feel that Burger does not address the more relevant and urgent question of illegally obtained handguns, which is more a criminal rather than a legislative issue.

5. The analogy is effective in that, as Burger states, "the right to keep and own an automobile is beyond question; equally beyond question is the power of the state to regulate the purchase or the transfer of such a vehicle and the right to license the vehicle and the driver with reasonable standards." However, as Burger also observes, the Constitution does not mention automobiles; therefore, the argument about the right to bear arms will always "stick" on the issue of Constitutional rights. It might be helpful for class discussion to engage in a comparison of the reasons for regulation of guns and the regulation of automobiles.

6. This question is open for discussion. His contextualization of the Second Amendment is very helpful; however, times have also changed significantly enough that most guns now owned and carried are often unregistered. Some may argue that by not addressing this large aspect of the issue, his argument is weakened.

ZERO TOLERANCE FOR SLAUGHTER

1. Tisdale is advocating for the complete ban of handguns and automatic weapons. At first, she wanted gun control, but after contemplation, she wants "gun elimination." She no longer feels that a compromise is the answer—she fears that too many children's lives are at stake.

2. Tisdale is referring to the second amendment of the U.S. Constitution and the intentions of its writers when drafting this document. The easy access to guns, coupled with gun-related school violence, is something she feels Franklin and Jefferson could never have anticipated.

Opponents could argue that Tisdale is making a presumption here—unsupportable because the drafters of the Constitution are dead.

3. Tisdale's list makes a compelling case on the surface. If we are prepared to regulate broccoli and stuffed animals, shouldn't we be doing the same for such dangerous items as guns? However, a pro-gun advocate could argue on several points 1) these items (broccoli and stuffed animals) are regulated, but not banned, as Tisdale proposes to do with guns; 2) these items are not actually protected under a constitutional amendment; 3) many guns require permits and registration, and there is some regulation on how they are manufactured.

4. The comment could be thrown right back at her "you can move."

5. Much of Tisdale's essay appeals to her audience's emotions—their desire to protect their children, their "babies." She also implies that it is dangerous to come out and speak against guns and gun owners—making them seem menacing. Her essay does an effective job, as long as her audience already agrees with her. At a debate, however, she leaves too many holes in her argument, as detailed in questions 2, 3, and 4.

6. They could undermine her argument because she begins her essay with a complete banning of all guns, and then makes allowances at the end. An opponent could jump on this concession. A single-shot rifle in the wrong hands would kill a child just as effectively as a handgun would.

AN ARMY OF GUN LIES

1. The first part of this question regards Kopel's claim of misleading statistics for gun-related child-death rates. Kopel argues that older

teens are also included in the rate, and, in fact, inflate the statistics because such teens are involved in illegal activities such as drug selling and robbery. A closer examination of the figures to which he does agree provides some interesting figures for discussion.

Addressing his concerns regarding inflated statistics, Kopel himself states that 2.6 children under the age of 14 are killed daily by guns, and .4 children under the age of 10. While the daily rate may seem small, when you add it up, it still equals 949 children under 14, and 146 children under 10 killed every year. If you take a middle figure from 13-17 children killed under the age of 18, say, 15, it still equals 5475 people under 18 killed every year by guns. Class discussion could address the ways we present statistical data to support arguments. Does his argument lose some of its impact when these larger numbers, drawn from his own data, are used?

Student answers will vary on the second part of the question. Does the fact that many older teens killed by guns are often engaged in illegal activities make their deaths less disturbing? Why or why not?

2. Although Kopel calls claims made against gun shows "audacious" lies, he does admit that person-to-person gun sales require no background checks. If a person happens to be selling a gun" at a gun show, the rules imposed on gun dealers are circumvented. A gun-control advocate can query, how many guns can such people who "happen to be selling a gun" actually sell before they are considered gun dealers? For the gun control advocate the issue is more that regardless of the rules imposed on gun dealers, gun sales without registration or background checks are happening at gun shows through such private ventures.

3. Student answers will vary but address whether these words effectively convey Kopel's feelings of injustice or whether they undermine his argument. Have students compare the actual "lie" he disputes to the

evidence he uses to dispute it to see if he indeed proves such "lies" "audacious" and "notorious."

4. Kopel feels that the entire story of Kellerman's study was not revealed by the media, such as the fact that ownership of burglar alarms could also be associated with an increased risk of death. Kopel also points out that Kellerman fails to note the fact that people who buy guns often live in high crime areas. What does this fact potentially do to the argument? Ask students to research the Kellerman study *(Gun Ownership as a Risk Factor for Homicide in the Home,* New England Journal of Medicine, vol. 329, No. 15, p. 1110) to see what their own opinions are of it.

5. The media, says Kopel, seems to be on the side of the antigun lobby based on the press time they give. In paragraphs 13-14, he explains how he feels the media is spreading lies. Why they do so is a bit more ambiguous. Perhaps because antigun stories are more sensational and controversial? Ask students to evaluate this media coverage for themselves for class discussion.

PHOTO: SHOE PROTEST

1. The shoes represent the missing people ripped from their lives by gun violence. Ask students to consider common sayings we have about shoes and feet—filling one's shoes, walking in another's shoes, knocked off your feet, etc. The shoes also leave two gaping holes in each pair—holes that we know should be filled with living feet. The emptiness of the holes serves as a reminder of the holes left in the social fabric, and the holes left in families and communities. Ask students to discuss if another article of clothing would be as symbolic.

2. There are many protests against gun violence featuring shouting people waving placards and angry fists. While a crowd of people does get attention, is also becomes common in a political area such as Washington D.C. Consider how much more is "said" by silent rows of empty shoes—no one is marching, waving, or shouting, because they can't. The shoes are reminders of the voices silenced. In many ways, the rows of shoes are more disturbing and send a more poignant message than any group of shouting protesters could.

3. Student answers will vary, but direct the class to explore the levels on which the photograph, and the action it depicts, operates. Include the power of imagery and symbolism in the discussion.

GUN CONTROL NEEDS A MIDDLE GROUND

1. Overall, Levin's approach seems to be reasoned and unbiased. For example, when discussing waiting periods, he notes that while waiting periods are unlikely to deter someone bent on killing another person from doing so (they just wait a bit longer to do it), gun waiting periods are likely to reduce impulse murders and suicides (people cool off). Gun control advocates might argue that middle ground is unreachable because Tisdale is a member of the "all-or-nothing" camp, a group that Levin says unable to engage in meaningful dialogue on this issue.

2. Levin sounds very reasoned and objective. He cites pros and cons for many of the issues he addresses. He also seems a bit concerned that the current debate is couched in "all or nothing" terms that preclude achieving any middle ground on the issue, something that he seems to find frustrating from both sides.

3. Student answers will vary.

4. Student answers will vary, but to facilitate this discussion, instructors may wish to break the class into groups with each researching the gun–related crime statistics from a particular state, Texas, Massachusetts, and the home state of your university or college.

5. This particular article appeared on a website that supported gun ownership. However, while the author appears to support gun ownership himself (he does not come out and say anything about banning weapons), he does see the need for waiting periods and gun education. He also admits that gun-related deaths are more likely to happen by accident than by design, implying that something must be done about this problem.

CAPITAL PUNISHMENT AND RETRIBUTION

A DEATH IN TEXAS

1. Student answers will vary, but it may seem ironic that a man scheduled to die soon is carefully watched to make sure he doesn't kill himself. Student discussion may address why it is important to the judicial process that he not take his own life.

2. Because Earle has been in jail himself, he can relate to some of the feelings Nobles has experienced. He also may be better able to see incarcerated individuals as real people, and not simply criminals. He is able to see past the reason for their incarceration to the person and personality involved. The relationship leads Earle to truly believe that people can change, and that Jon Nobles is one such person.

3. Nobles seems resigned to his imminent death. He feels truly remorseful for his crimes on an emotional and spiritual level. The fact that he has become religious may also add a dimension to his readiness to die and

the profound personality change he has experienced. Student answers will vary on the second part of the question.

4. The final portion of Earle's essay is like a countdown. Hour by hour, minute by minute, we are led through the last moments of a human life. Students may have different reactions to this dramatic technique, but most are likely to agree that it leaves an impression on the reader.

5. Earle remains distant from making any moral judgments on Nobles' crime, or his ultimate punishment for most of his essay. It is only in his final paragraph, in his closing comments, that we get a clear message from Earle regarding rehabilitation, crime, and Jon Nobles. "I do know that Jon Nobles changed profoundly while he was in prison. [...] Given as many people as we lock up, we better learn to rehabilitate someone. I believe Jon might have been able to teach us how. Now we'll never know." The impression we are left with is one of loss—society's loss—for what we could have learned and how we could have benefited.

A RECKONING ON DEATH ROW

1. Student answers will vary but Alter's comments imply that he is an educated, serious person who assumes the same of his audience. He seems to take political and legal issues seriously and from an informed position. His comment about Jagger and Jackson also implies that he is not swayed by the opinions of pop stars or political pundits.

2. Alter is making an assumption that his audience will not only know who Heller and Kafka are, but will also be familiar with their work. Ask students to research these two writers if they are unfamiliar with them.

3. Alter is concerned that "full-and-fair" doesn't really exist, despite what Bush claims. He explains that many appeals are never heard, and cases are not formally revisited. In his opinion, when a person's life is on the line, he feels that the courts have an obligation to address their request.

4. Student answers will vary.

5. Have students research this issue and the current policies regarding DNA appeals for a class discussion.

ALTER FALTERS

1. While Alter does indeed call for a *moratorium* on the death penalty, a moratorium is not an outright ban. In fact, Alter goes out of his way to establish that he is not against the death penalty in principle or in practice in cases of certain guilt. He is objecting to denials made to death row prisoners requesting DNA tests. Pambianco may be skewing the information to make his point.

2. Pambianco believes that the issue should be whether the death penalty is morally wrong. He makes the statement that the issue isn't about innocence, "nor should it be." Student answers will vary, but some may express confusion about why innocence *isn't* the issue.

3. Student answers will vary, but class discussion may address whether Pambianco's examples are parallel to the situation of death row inmates wrongfully being put to death. How likely is the legal system to admit that some casualties happen? Americans like to believe that their legal system protects them from such error, and that justice is fair. Pambianco seems to imply that nothing is perfect, and we must accept that there will be some fatal errors along the way, but that is the sacrifice we must make.

4. Student answers will vary.

5. Pambianco objects to the idea that the controversy over the death penalty can be couched in any other terms but moral ones. Alter is likely to disagree.

CARTOON: DNA AND THE ELECTRIC CHAIR

1. The cartoonist is arguing that DNA evidence should be allowed before a death row inmate is executed, presumably if that inmate wishes it. DNA evidence after the fact is useless.

2. The cartoon is making a statement about DNA evidence, so it presumes that the audience will understand what such evidence is and as well as the current controversy surrounding it.

3. The people in the drawing are expressionless and formless. They are secondary to the message and the moment.

THE PLACE FOR VENGEANCE

1. The authors express concern that adherence to the law for civil reasons and social order is being superceded by emotional appeals for revenge. The idea that the killer is punished to give closure to the victim's family is getting greater voice than the idea that the killer should pay because of a wrong against society. Students may address if they agree that this is a troubling shift, or a logical one.

2. Many witnesses express that the suffering of the executed felon is nothing compared to what the killer did to their loved one. The

119

punishment doesn't fit the crime. For it to fit, killers would have to plead for their lives, have hope that they might live and still die anyway, and feel terror and pain. Some witnesses feel that the killers just get off "too easy." Student answers will vary but they may discuss the psychological impact of a witness indeed getting what they want—watching the death of the killer as they feel it should be, slow and terrifying.

3. The grieving process is more difficult for the friends and loved ones of a murder victim because they are not allowed to grieve and heal. Instead, they face a long, drawn out process of trials, appeals, hearings, and finally, they may witness the death of their loved one's killer. Witnessing the death of the convicted may reopen old wounds, and cause another layer of emotional stress and turmoil.

4. Many Americans fear that if the death penalty is not pursued (in states that allow only the death penalty, not life in prison), there is a good chance that the killer could be paroled. Thus, they are forced to make a choice—support the death penalty or face the possibility the killer will walk away someday.

5. Student answers will vary.

6. Student answers will vary.

*Please reference the book's Companion Website, **Dialogues on the Web**, at (www.ablongman.com/goshgarian) for additional class activities and questions, topical resources, links to research and reference pages, online writing labs, and updates to links listed in the book. Also see its "Instructor Resources" section providing teaching, writing, and research links.*

CHAPTER SIXTEEN
MORAL ISSUES IN MEDICINE

STEM CELL RESEARCH

BRAVE NEW WORLD

1. There are many issues facing the science connected with this technology. In addition to the issues outlined in this article, students may wish to research one or several of them for class discussion. Stem cell research: Embryonic stem cells hold the most promise for curing many diseases. Such cells are cultivated from donated human embryos left over from IVF. But it is these cell lines that are the source of the controversy in the political, social, and scientific arenas today.

   Cloning: While Dolly the sheep was cloned to help facilitate drug discovery and gene therapy, some scientists have opened up more controversial issues by vowing to try to clone human beings as a reproductive option. Students should also review the essays included in Chapter 17's casebook for a more in depth look at human cloning.

   Genetic engineering: Could we have designer babies? The possibility becomes more plausible as we learn more about what our genes do. In addition to helping cure or eliminate genetic diseases, genetic engineering carries controversial applications of choosing desirable genetic traits.

2. Trefil explains that in-vitro fertilization (IVF), used by infertile couples to conceive a child, often creates "extra" embryos. It is what happens to these embryos that is a central issue to the stem cell debate. These embryos can be donated for stem cell research, but some people object to such experimentation on the grounds that because embryos have the potential to become living people, it is unethical to use them for research. Moreover, they don't want the government (through the NIH) to fund such research with their tax dollars. Cloning these embryos may hold the key to extending the existing approved stem cell lines to pursue promising lines of research.

3. Life used to be as simple as the "birds and the bees," but IVF and the test tube baby introduced a new set of reproductive options and issues. What happens to "left over" embryos? Can we someday clone our loved ones or ourselves? If we are infertile, can we use DNA from other cells to create a baby? Should we use genetic research to ensure that our children do not have preventable genetic diseases? Can we take such research to the next level, and pick embryos that have certain traits, such as blue eyes, or brown hair?

4. Pluripotent cells have the potential to become any cell—a neuron, blood cell, muscle tissue—whereas adult stem cells lack this flexibility. Only embryonic stem cells retain pluripotent qualities.

5. Student answers will vary, but the potential to cure so many devastating diseases, including Parkinson's, makes a compelling case.

6. The author seems to sense the potential for some of this research, but is against other lines, such as human cloning.

REMARKS BY THE PRESIDENT ON STEM CELL RESEARCH

1. Student answers will vary.

2. The speech provides some fundamental information about the issue. By keeping the science and issues as simple as possible, the speech has a greater chance of reaching a wider audience.

3. Student answers will vary.

4. The cloning discussion seems to be out of place. However, it may have been included because the two issues are so often associated with each other. Compare the comments made in the speech with information provided by Trefil and in Chapter 17.

5. He does address the issue in his speech, but side steps it by explaining that NIH funding would only support research on existing stem cell

lines. New lines, regardless of the wishes of the "parents" of the embryos to be destroyed, will not be supported by government funding.

A QUESTION OF LIFE OR DEATH

1. Student answers will vary but Woodward would probably note Bush's stance that life comes from "the Creator" and therefore have a religious leaning. Have students identify the words Bush uses to describe the embryos (egg, snowflake, seeds), and discuss what these words reveal about the President's position.

2. In paragraph 2, Woodward states "The ethical questions then become clear: what values should we place on human embryos, and how should their well-being be balanced with that of the millions whose acute suffering might be alleviated through stem cell research and development?" The issue is compounded by the fact that these embryos are going to be destroyed anyway.

3. See Chapter 2 for a discussion on slippery slope arguments. The Catholic Church position is that the IVF is morally wrong because it creates extra embryos, which the Catholic Church regards as human life from the moment of conception. The argument is if you make distinctions between when human life deserves protection, where is the line drawn?

4. Woodward advocates a middle ground. He wants to pursue promising lines of research, but not at the expense of medical ethics.

REASON, FAITH, AND STEM CELLS

1. Kinsley's tone in his opening paragraph is sarcastic. His second sentence is absurd—which is the feeling he wishes to convey to his readers—the new rules concerning stem cell research are as absurd as the "conditions" he details.

2. Kinsley explains that the compromise really isn't much of one. He feels that living humans are being made to needlessly suffer in favor of an ambiguous argument over when life begins and when human life should be protected. In paragraphs 8, 9, and 10 he further describes why he feels that the argument over the beginning of life is a false issue.

3. Absolutism, as described in paragraph 5, bases its argument on "if you don't protect every human being from the moment of conception, where do you draw the line?" Compare this argument to the slippery slope argument the Catholic Church makes against IVF and the "extra" embryos it creates described by Woodward in the previous essay. The weakness of the argument is that it implies that one life is equally as valuable as another—a fact the author disputes as not only illogical, but unreasonable. Furthermore, it implies that an embryo, which has the potential for human life, deserves greater consideration than an existing life—such as a person with Parkinson's disease.

4. If Kinsley is going to argue that the anti-stem cell debate isn't based on reason, he must prove otherwise by making a logical and reasonable argument himself. Otherwise, he would be guilty of the same transgression of which he accuses his opponents.

ABORTION

ABORTION IN AMERICAN HISTORY

1. Student answers will vary, but some may argue that the debate can be intensely personal and very direct. Authors Minnick and Howley, for example, are unlikely to agree with her assessment. Quindlen, however, discusses abortion in more abstract, yet still personal, terms, so she may be more likely to relate to Pollitt's point of view.

   Judith Jarvis Thomson's famous violinist attempts to demonstrate that it is not necessarily true that one person's right to life outweighs another person's right to control what happens to her body when these rights come into conflict. Her example presents a scenario in which a person's right to control what happens to her body outweighs another person's right to life. The example reads, "Suppose you wake up one morning and find that a famous violinist's circulatory system has been plugged into yours, so that your kidneys can be used to extract poisons from her blood as well as from your own. She needs to remain plugged into you for nine months. If you unplug her, she will die because there is no other person who has the right blood type. Here is a clear situation in which the violinist's right to life comes into conflict with your right to control what happens to your own body. Is it morally permissible for you to unplug the violinist--given that you know that she will die when you do so?"

2. Pollitt assumes that readers will be familiar with this moral argument, or be ambitious enough to find out more about it. Readers unfamiliar with this case may be confused, but failure to explain the example more explicitly does not detract from the overall message of Pollitt's essay.

3. Student answers may vary, but it is likely that many students will be surprised enough by this number to possibly dispute it. There is a general feeling that abortion is a 20th century phenomenon, and that it wasn't practiced much in previous eras.

4. Pollitt uses the book, and much of the historical information it contains, to support her own argument in favor of abortion. Pollitt's position is that not only should abortions be protected as a woman's right, but also that the information in Reagan's book proves that outlawing abortion is unlikely to stop the practice, just make it more deadly.

5. She supports this statement with data that in the 1920's "some 15,000 women a year died from abortions." When abortion was legalized, material mortality rates plummeted...in New York State alone they dropped 45 percent. So while the statement itself hinges on opinion,

she is able to provide other facts that imply that it may be true—from the perspective she is arguing.

6. Student answers will vary but have students review the items Pollitt lists in her final paragraph: 1) how free should women be to have sexual experiences without the threat of unwanted pregnancy, 2) how much right should they have to make their own decisions, 3) how subordinate should they be to men, etc.

ABORTION IS NOT THE ANSWER—EVER

1. Minnick takes a hard line position on abortion. He calls it murder, plain and simple, and says that an abortion is not acceptable, even in more "socially accepted" situations of rape. He does not address the related issue of cases of life threatening situations to the mother. Ask students to consider what his position in such cases is likely to be, and why.

2. Minnick's story is compelling, if not a bit overly dramatized. Paragraphs 1-10 relates what a typical couple facing this decision probably goes through. Paragraphs 11 and 12 dramatizes the situation "joined emotionally by their love and physically by their arms..." but makes Minnick's story appealing. He is the result of their decision. He would not exist if the doctor had been on time, his father followed the rules, or his mother didn't take a chance.

3. Minnick, a self-declared Democrat, separates his viewpoint from religious, political, and social arguments because he feels this is the stance that is most compelling. People can hold different religious, political, and social viewpoints, but all are a part of humanity. Students may discuss whether he makes a successful argument on the "humanity" grounds.

4. Minnick's statement in paragraph 17 is a common point of dispute. A point that he fails to support with logical proof. "The fetus has cells,

126

which multiply and grow, thus it's a living organism and it's a person." It is the final part of the sentence that is disputable. Opponents could argue that other living organisms have cells, which multiply and grow, but these organisms are not people.

5. Minnick is taking the position that abortion is not permissible—ever. He is consistent throughout his essay, arguing that the life of the unborn child should supercede any emotional, intellectual, or financial anguish it may cause the mother. Students may agree that his consistent position makes his argument more compelling. However, they may also argue about the emotional state of rape victims—an issue Minnick does not address. He states, "For the woman, the burden of rape would be heavy enough. And an abortion would only hurt her more emotionally and physically." This is an enormous assumption on his part, and may weaken his argument. Ask students to discuss whether his argument would be stronger if this paragraph (22) were left out.

ADVERTISEMENT: NATIONAL ABORTION FEDERATION

1. Student answers will vary.

2. Student answers will vary, but point out the fact that the actual pill is not depicted, or anything else that is related to the advertisement, the "product," or the counseling service the ad promotes. The ad is non-confrontational, and understated.

3. The woman depicted in the ad is young and professional looking. She does not look like an immature teen, or the sort of person who makes decisions lightly. She is not "sexy" looking in a glamorous way, although she is attractive and nicely dressed. The audience is likely to mirror what this woman represents—young, professional, secure women who are open to this choice.

4. Student answers will vary.

5. Student answers will vary, but ask students to consider what the objective of the ad really is. Would students respond to it by visiting the NAF website? Discuss.

THE MYTH OF THE PRO-CHOICE WOMAN

1. There tends to be an association between pro-choice and liberals, democrats, and, in the case of the man who made the statement, young women. Students should discuss why such assumptions exist.

2. Howley feels that such men are "disgusting" and cowardly. It is ironic that she believes that the man at the party thinks she is pro-choice because she is a young woman, yet she makes sweeping assumptions about men throughout the essay.

3. Howley's introduction is likely to draw in her readers because it starts with conflict. We want to find out what she is going to say. The hope is that we will continue to read on to find out why she finds men who assume this position on abortion so "disgusting."

4. The title implies that women aren't really pro-choice. Her essay continues this line of reasoning by asserting that women are "steered" to abortion clinics by male pressure. Men don't want to be held accountable for their sexual mistakes.

5. Student answers will vary, but this statement positions Howley as a Catholic who would have religious reasons for being anti-abortion as well as social and personal ones.

SOME THOUGHTS ABOUT ABORTION

1. In paragraph 7, Quindlen writes, "I believe that in a contest between the living and the almost living, the latter must, if necessary, give way to the will of the former. That is what the fetus is to me, the almost

living." Her own pregnancies as well of those of young people she has counseled led her to this conclusion.

2. In paragraph 10, Quindlen questions the moral right to choose abortion when a pregnancy is inconvenient, when one can support a child financially and emotionally. Legally, she always wants the right to choose, but she wonders about the morality of such a decision.

3. The form of this argument is closer to an inductive argument than a deductive one because Quindlen begins the article with examples that lead up to her conclusions.

4. Student answers will vary.

5. No, the essay would likely lose much of its power if Quindlen simply used factual examples, quoted from other people's experiences and research, or referred to authorities from both sides of the issue. Quindlen is dealing with feelings and ideas, not with provable facts.

6. Quindlen's claim comes at the end of paragraph 4: "And that is where I find myself now, in the middle, hating the idea of abortion, hating the idea of having them outlawed." Refinement of this claim occurs when Quindlen questions an abortion simply for the sake of convenience.

7. Paragraph 8 seems to be the turning point in the essay. Although she stated her position in paragraph 4—"reality is something in the middle. And that is where I find myself now, in the middle. And that is where I find myself now, in the middle, hating the idea of abortion, hating the idea of having them outlawed"—she develops this idea further by questioning the ideas of abortion for convenience. Her husband's comment and her description of the potential baby's characteristics (blue eyes, red hair, with athletic ability) all reinforce her view that abortion may not be morally defensible though it should be legally available.

PHYSICIAN-ASSISTED SUICIDE AND END OF LIFE CHOICES

THE SUPREME COURT AND PHYSICIAN-ASSISTED SUICIDE

1. Angell makes the comparison to Roe v. Wade because assisted suicide is a nationwide debate that she believes involves a personal choice similar in nature to abortion. Abortion and assisted suicide are similar in that both involve the individual choice of taking a human life. They differ in that the life taken in one instance is a person enduring a terminally ill disease and the other is an unborn life without conscious choice. Students can discuss the similarities and differences they see between the two. Angell may have made this connection because the legality of the choice involved is similar. The patient/pregnant woman is making a decision not to prolong a life.

2. Paragraphs 6 and 7 differentiate the active and passive roles of doctors and patients in assisted suicide and euthanasia. Making a distinction is important because of the moral ambiguity that surrounds the decisions/actions of both. For both the goal is to end suffering, but as she reminds readers euthanasia can be performed without the patient's knowledge and participation. Assisted suicide requires the patient's knowledge and participation.

3. The abuses feared are as follows: Assisted suicide would be a threat to the economically and socially vulnerable. The poor, disabled, and elderly might be coerced to request it. Overburdened families or cost conscious doctors might pressure vulnerable patients to request suicide. Angell's statement that "no human endeavor is immune to abuses" is one to consider as satisfactory, especially since the Roe v. Wade decision did not have such an abusive outcome.

4. Angell uses her story about her father to make an abstract issue concrete, although students could argue that *any* example could have done this. Students can discuss whether or not Angell is credible as a writer when saying, "I have no doubt my father would have chosen [physician-assisted suicide]." Could she know this for certain?

5. Students can argue Angell's statement, "If there is to be assisted suicide, doctors must not be involved." How is this possible? Although we can recognize Angell's points that it is the patient's decision and the patient should not be denied the opportunity to end "unbearable suffering," doctors, according to the Hippocratic Oath, should still play an active role in their patient's care. Students can debate over how much decision-making involvement they would want doctors to have.

DEATH AND DIGNITY—A CASE OF INDIVIDUALIZED DECISION MAKING

1. Student answers will vary.

2. Both Diane and Tim are diagnosed with leukemia and given a 25 percent chance of survival. The immediate reactions are the same but their ultimate decisions about treatment differ. Diane asks for the Hemlock Society's "recipe" two weeks after her initial diagnosis. While it seems both doctor-patient relationships were familiar ones and based on honesty, Diane and Quill were quicker to come to an understanding about her future life with the disease. As paragraph 6 of the Hendlin article suggests, he and Tim took longer to discuss things in an open manner.

3. Open to discussion. Neither Quill nor Angell give readers the details of where and who would be with the patient during the final moments of an in-hospital physician-assisted suicide. It seems there would be a closer monitoring than Diane's hour alone at home.

4. Quill only indirectly made Diane's suicide possible because he was more of a friend/confidant. While he was sure to offer medical advice, he allowed her all the decision-making power. He did not impose his advice on her; as the title of his article suggests, this was a case of *individualized* decision-making. We can gather that Quill is for the legalization of physician-assisted suicide from paragraphs 7 and 14

131

where he admits he will take any risks for the patients he really knows and cares about.

PHOTO: AGED HANDS

1. Student answers will vary.

2. Student answers will vary.

3. Student answers will vary, but ask students to consider how the photo could be interpreted in different contexts.

SUICIDE, ASSISTED SUICIDE, AND MEDICAL ILLNESS

1. Student answers will vary.

2. Terminally ill patients generally fear becoming burdens on their families and they anticipate future suffering. The opening paragraph describes Tim's immediate reaction and his request for support in carrying out his suicide. "He was worried about becoming dependent and feared both the symptoms of his disease and the side effects of treatment.

3. As Tim's case suggests, there is often a preceding inability to share feelings or handle depression. Terminally ill patients need to feel wanted and that they are still valuable members of society, not just sick people in need of medical care.

4. Open to discussion. Students can create a list of reasons why doctors need/want to maintain control and compare it to a list of reasons why patients might feel a similar need/want of control. The "real issue" for patients is fear, which needs to be handled by caring physicians appropriately. In essence, frustration cannot take over. Doctors and patients must have an open dialogue.

5. If life is defined as a "pursuit of happiness," it will not change when referring to the terminally ill as long as the patient, like Tim, takes advantage of his remaining days to be honest and open with family and friends. Hendlin's use of this quote infers the need to do something to give meaning to life, which is applicable to both the healthy and the terminally ill.

FINAL RIGHTS

1. Student answers will vary. The fact that Carmichael's friend saw her own husband, a person she dearly loved, waste away and suffer makes her more resolved not to follow the same route. Knowing this fact may help readers understand her point of view.

2. At first, Carmichael agrees to her friend's request, partly because she is caught off guard, partly out of loyalty, and partly because she agrees that her friend has the right to make this choice. She later realizes that she can't allow her friend to jump out the window of her apartment, not because she doesn't believe in her friend's reasons for doing so, but because she is concerned for her neighbors and herself. "Could I sleep in my room after my friend plunged to her death from my window? Could I enter and leave passing the place where her crumpled body had lain?"

3. As question 2 also addresses, Carmichael considers the feelings of others—herself, her neighbors, and people passing on the street. Her friend is more concerned with herself—probably a natural stance to take considering the circumstances.

4. Student answers will vary.

5. The name of her friend is not important, the point of her narrative is that her friend had to make this choice, alone, and unassisted, because she had no other options. She could be anybody's friend.

6. Carmichael wonders what choices she will be forced to make herself. And she is troubled by the fact that her friend had to make such a desperate, violent choice.

*Please reference the book's Companion Website, **Dialogues on the Web**, at (www.ablongman.com/goshgarian) for additional class activities and questions, topical resources, links to research and reference pages, online writing labs, and updates to links listed in the book. Also see its "Instructor Resources" section providing teaching, writing, and research links.*

CHAPTER SEVENTEEN
CASEBOOK: THE HUMAN CLONING DEBATE

EMBRYOS ARE US

1. The cartoon conveys the artist's view that the private sector is driven by financial gain at the expense of quality and by extension, safety. The private sector is likely to cut corners in order to "offer" this technology to the public. Because the salesman is such a shady character, we can presume that nothing that comes out of his mouth is truthful.

2. The salesman is a slick and shady character—miss matched clothing, "villain" style moustache, and huge grinning teeth. He looks like a used car salesman—and that is the point. Everything about the salesman and his surroundings says "cheap."

3. The artist assumes that his audience will understand the visual cues he uses. The car salesman image, the "K-Mart" blue light special, the balloons and banners. International readers would probably perceive that there is something "off" about the salesman, but may miss the other cues that convey that the merchandise is cheap and of low quality.

4. We expect this guy to be selling used cars, or a cheap kitchen gadget or quick fix product. With petri dishes stacked up high, the artist twists the car salesman cliché to fit the issue and concern of human cloning. Ask students to read paragraph 48 in the next article by Gibbs and compare what the business person says to the image of this cartoon.

BABY, IT'S YOU, AND YOU AND YOU....

1. Gibbs gives many reasons why people are interested in human cloning throughout the essay. Students may evaluate which ones, if any, seem more reasonable than others. Most researchers are interested in applying cloning technology—not actual cloning of humans—to find

cures and therapies for disease, develop new drugs, and even grow organs and tissues for replacement (not a whole human to "harvest," but individual organs). The general population has a wide range of responses, many based on misconceptions about what human cloning can and cannot do. In this essay, it seems that science wants cures, and people want replacements.

2. Paragraphs 7 & 8 describe some fears scientists have of a backlash against this technology. They are concerned that if a few renegade scientists, bent on fame, try to clone humans, the results could be devastating and the technology banned altogether. Thus, many promising lines of research could be stopped because of the transgressions of a few.

3. The primary misconception people seem to harbor is that a clone baby would be an exact replica of the DNA donor. One man thinks he would know what his clone would like and dislike. Another feels that cloning technology could make him "immortal." Some parents think it could "resurrect" their dead children. One family even thinks that cloning their mother would give her a "second chance" to live a better life, because her first one was so hard. Scientists repeatedly explain that a clone is not a duplicate. Chemical factors in utero, environmental factors at birth, and simple life experience all leave a mark that makes us individuals. And a clone is a separate person, with separate desires, wants, needs, and thoughts—just as an identical twin is not a duplicate of his or her sibling.

4. The "purists" at either end do not seem to grapple with any moral, ethical, political, or social arguments. Cloning is either completely wrong, or completely right. For example, the Catholic Church says that it is wrong because it is meddling with God's will. Advocates for human cloning say it isn't an issue of ethics—the medical technology makes it a reproductive option that we should use. Student answers will vary on the final part of the question, but ask students to explain where they stand—are they purists, or in the middle?

136

5. Student answers will vary, but as Wilmut indicates in paragraph 24, the likelihood of success is minute. Do the ends justify the means? A parallel line of questioning may stimulate class discussion. Would the FDA allow a drug on the market that could affect a complete cure of a disease, but would do so in only 1 out of every 277 patients?

6. Paragraph 24 explains Dorner's stance that he wouldn't mind being part of such an experiment. However, the risk to Dorner is only that he would give up a few cells. The risk to the clone, however, is much greater. Most students would agree that the true guinea pig is the clone. Bioethicist Kass in paragraph 35 explains, "no one is looking at this from the point of view of the clone."

7. Student answers will vary.

CLONING AND THE HUMAN SELF

1. To Raymo, the success rate, 1 out of 277 attempts, seemed to preclude anyone from trying this technology on a human being. The odds were just too steep, and to him, the risk of creating deformed children seemed too great. He changed his mind six months later when he read that some scientists, such as Panos Zavos, had announced their intentions to actually try it.

2. Raymo's essay is less of an argument than an exploration of the idea of human cloning and its relationship to our sense of individuality and self. To Raymo, cloning is not replicating. You cannot duplicate a life of experiences. He is troubled by what this technology will mean to our sense of identity.

3. In paragraphs 14 & 15, Raymo explains what he thinks makes up the "self." "A self is also a rich store of conscious and unconscious memories. [...] In principle, it is information too [...] information embodied in that flux of flowing matter called life, partly inborn, partly acquired through experience."

4. Student answers will vary, but Raymo's perspective is highly analytical and circumvents many of the moral and ethical arguments currently circulating and focuses on the more technical aspects of what it means to be a "self" – and what determines individuality.

HUMAN CLONING—JUST DON'T SAY NO

1. Student answers will vary, but the "yuk factor" is a real phrase used in science. William Bains, author of "Biotechnology from A to Z" defines the "yuk factor" as "a flippant term for the very real observation that the public, and indeed many scientists, judge the ethical acceptability of experimental procedures and biological manipulations with a scale of distaste. Thus, the creation of a cloned carrot in the 1960s was greeted with amusement by the press, the first frog in the early 1970s with interest and some caution, and the creation of Dolly in 1997 resulted in widespread alarm." The "yuk factor" can also be tied into the risks of the procedure. Many cloned lamb fetuses were miscarried, and others born so malformed that they were euthanized immediately. What might a human fetus face?

2. While Macklin argues that the parents are likely to love the child as much as the first, is this love for the new child, or for its dead sibling? The child will know that he or she was not wanted as a new individual, but as a replacement for a dearly loved lost sibling. The physiological impact may be great.

3. Student answers will vary, but in addition to some of the information provided in the answer to question 2, ask students to consider the perspective of both the grieving parent and the cloned child.

4. Student answers will vary, but again, while we don't ban something simply because it is distasteful, there is no proof that no harm exists. Do we have to prove harm before we ban something? Or is there a place for argument and logic based on past experiments?

CREEPY AND INEVITABLE: CLONING US

1. Student answers will vary, but ask students to explain what "playing God" really means. Is it an expression that makes sense only to religious people, or does it have universally understood implications?

2. Student answers will vary. In his introduction, Pertman briefly identifies some parallels between the two technologies. In both procedures, fertilization happens outside the body, and requires implantation of the embryo, either into the egg-donor mother, or a surrogate. While IVF faced some similar concerns as human cloning, it still required that the basic components of reproduction be a sperm and an egg. Human cloning allows parents to skip the component of a sperm altogether.

3. Student answers will vary, but the general opinion, as expressed in this essay and in others from this section, is that scientists who pursue human cloning are doing so for selfish reasons—they want the fame and recognition of being the first to claim success. They are not considering the embryo's role in this. Pertman explains in paragraph 19, "Experiments...often fail. Thousands of animals died before and after birth, emerged deformed, developed physical and neurological abnormalities, and exhibited all sorts of other small and large problems before Dolly the cloned sheep arrived in 1997." What do we do with the failed experiments? Will we even know about them?

4. Student answers will vary but class discussion can address the question if human cloning is truly inevitable, as several authors in this casebook indicate, then is it more practical to try to regulate the process rather than outright ban it? Or are the same people likely to ignore the ban also likely to circumvent regulatory practices?

139

HUMAN CLONING ISN'T AS SCARY AS IT SOUNDS

1. At the end of his first paragraph, Wachbroit states that the danger is not the technology itself, but "in the misunderstanding of its significance." The rest of his essay addresses reasons why cloning probably won't happen, and if it did, why it isn't really so bad. He fails, however, to explain the full meaning of this sentence, which seems to imply that he will explain exactly what the *significance* of human cloning really is.

2. Student answers will vary, but Wachbroit repeats many of the misconceptions regarding human cloning—that it will provide an exact replica of the original DNA source, that it can confer immortality, and that it can duplicate a dead child. Unlike other authors in this section, Wachbroit dismisses the threat of people actually attempting cloning because it is too difficult. For example, he states in paragraph 5 that once parents understand that they can't bring back the exact child they lost, they are unlikely to persist. As other authors in this casebook reveal, however, some parents are undeterred by this knowledge.

3. In several points in his essay, such as paragraph 4, 5, and 8, Wachbroit indicates that reason will overtake hubris. He believes that the complications of cloning will deter most people. The interesting thing is that he keeps referring to the decision to clone or not to clone as a parental one. Is the future of human cloning really in the hands of prospective parents, or egotistical researchers?

4. Student answers will vary.

5. In paragraph 2, Wachbroit explains that genetic determinism is the view that genes determine everything about us, exclusive of environmental factors that act upon us. Most scientists do not believe in genetic determinism—the evidence suggests that even small chemical changes in fetal environment can influence what genes are expressed. Outside the womb, daily interactions with events and environment also shape the individual—diet, health, stimulus—all

influence who we are and what we look like. Paragraph 11 also addresses genetic determinism. Wachbroit's point is that because genetic determinism is inherently false, many of the more repugnant reasons people may have pursued cloning become non-issues.

6. In his concluding paragraph, Wachbroit admits that he does not wish to dismiss the ethical concerns" raised by people regarding reproductive technologies. He just feels that banning cloning will not resolve the issue.

SHOULD HUMAN CLONING BE PERMITTED?

1. Have students look up the word integrity to make sure everyone understands what Baird means. In paragraph 5, Baird states "Making children by cloning means that [children] do not have [a] dual genetic origin; they are not connected to others in the same biological way as the rest of humanity." She continues in paragraph 7, "Cloning directs the production of human beings in an unprecedented way." In paragraph 9, she observes, "Reproduction by nuclear-transfer cloning makes it possible to think about genetically enhancing humans. [...] If it works, it is likely to be used more often than just occasionally."

Human cloning changes the way we view how reproduction can happen, who needs to be involved, and what we must leave up to chance. Currently, reproduction carries certain assumptions. While we may use different methods to reproduce, such as IVF, we still depend on mixed genetic information from a male and a female. The integrity of the DNA remains constant. With cloning technology, genes may be altered—and once introduced, such alterations may indeed affect the "integrity" of reproduction. Transgenic individuals may pass altered genetic information to their offspring, and we can't predict the outcome generations later.

2. Student answers will vary.

141

3. In paragraph 5, Baird explains that an aboriginal group in Canada (this is actually practiced by many American Indian tribes) said "when they had to make a big decision in their community, they always considered what the consequences were likely to be in the seventh generation." The rule is extremely applicable to the human cloning argument because the decisions we make now could have significant ramifications on future generations, and there is no way to "undo" genetic manipulation once it has entered the gene pool. Have the class approach the issue as a "tribe" to discuss whether they will allow this technology into their "community."

4. Student answers will vary.

5. Student answers will vary but ask students to review Baird's specific concerns outlined in paragraph 4 regarding how children would fit into society and how they would feel about themselves.

6. Baird fears that only people with the financial resources to pursue this line of reproduction will do so. What sort of traits would this group wish to enhance? We would be "taking human evolution into our own hands." Baird doubts that we are "wise enough" to handle the social consequences.

7. Student answers will vary.

8. Baird's conclusion begins in paragraph 17. In her introduction, she cites data that indicates that 90% of people in democratic societies are opposed to human cloning. As such, this is a social issue, separate from the ethical and medical arguments that are circulating. In paragraph 17, she states that cloning "is a matter of social policy [because it will] shape society for our children, their children, and after." She also notes, "Concerns about individual and social harms from cloning are strong enough that it is not justified to permit it." She makes a solid argument, but whether students agree with her reasons is up to individual debate.

YES, HUMAN CLONING SHOULD BE PERMITTED

1. In paragraph 2, MacDonald expresses his concern that banning something because a majority is opposed to it is dangerous. He concedes in his next paragraph that his analogy may be flawed, because human cloning carries risks and possible harmful effects. But his example raises an interesting question—ask the class to discuss the limits of popular opinion. Does a democracy allow for the desires of a minority to supercede the wishes of the majority?

2. Baird is likely to point out that because no human clones have been made, it is impossible to truly determine what harm they may or may not suffer. However, her argument is framed on the idea that if it could cause probable harm, you shouldn't pursue it simply because that harm is not absolutely proven. Other authors against banning cloning are likely to agree with his position, having expressed similar sentiments.

3. MacDonald does not argue against all of Baird's comments. Specifically, he does not address Baird's concerns that once we alter the gene pool, there is no turning back. He does address her "majority rule" argument and her concerns regarding the psychological implications to the cloned child and human identity. Student answers will vary, but he does a fair job addressing these issues specifically in paragraphs 3, 4, and 5.

4. MacDonald is arguing against an outright ban, and more specifically, that Baird has not created a sufficiently compelling argument justifying such a ban. He is advocating for regulation and exploration.

5. Student answers will vary but the fact that Baird is a geneticist and a medical professional does lend some credibility to her argument, and may weaken MacDonald's stance when he attempts to argue medical points. However, much of Baird's argument is framed in terms of benefits and risks to society and to the psychology of the child. Does the fact that she is not a psychologist weaken her argument?

*Please reference the book's Companion Website, **Dialogues on the Web**, at (www.ablongman.com/goshgarian) for additional class activities and questions, topical resources, links to research and reference pages, online writing labs, and updates to links listed in the book. Also see its "Instructor Resources" section providing teaching, writing, and research links.*